BURT FRANKLIN: RESEARCH & SOURCE WORKS SERIES 604
Essays in Literature & Criticism 103

A STUDY IN CORNEILLE

CORNEILLE.

A STUDY IN CORNEILLE

BY

LEE DAVIS LODGE, A. M.,

BURT FRANKLIN
NEW YORK

842
C81xlo

71-2321

Published by LENOX HILL Pub. & Dist. Co. (Burt Franklin)
235 East 44th St., New York, N.Y. 10017
Originally Published: 1891
Reprinted: 1970
Printed in the U.S.A.

S.B.N.: 8337-2133X
Library of Congress Card Catalog No.: 70-132812
Burt Franklin: Research and Source Works Series 604
Essays in Literature and Criticism 103

Reprinted from the original edition in the Princeton University
Library.

To My Wife.

PREFACE.

THE purpose of this little book is, as Mr. Vellum would say, twofold: The writer has endeavored to prepare a work from which American readers unacquainted with the French language may obtain something like a fair conception of the life, genius and character of " Le grand Corneille."

"Something like a fair conception "—the words are used advisedly, for the writer, who has for years lived in close companionship with the works of the subject of his sketch, knows full well how feeble, unsatisfactory and inadequate is this attempt to exhibit the grandeur and the sublimity of the noblest dramatist of France.

Translating a poem, like subjecting a flower to the chemist's art, may preserve the perfume, but it must needs annihilate the form. It is thought, however, that to know Corneille in English may be better than not to know him at all.

The second aim had in view has been to furnish to advanced students of French a trustworthy sketch of the evolution of the drama, the advent of Corneille, the historic function he performed and the character of his genius.

The passages here translated have been rendered very literally in order to keep, as nearly as might be, the exact thought of the poet.

This work makes no pretence whatever at being a complete account of Corneille; it is simply a tribute to his transcendant genius, and a modest effort to win for him the homage that is his due.

In conclusion the writer wishes to express his grateful thanks to Mr. Edward Farquhar, the learned Assistant Librarian of the United States Patent Office, who has aided him much by critically reading all of the proof, and to his colleague, counsellor and friend, Prof. J. Howard Gore, B. S., Ph. D., who has generously encouraged him in his labors, wisely advised him in his perplexities and continually rendered him sympathetic assistance of value too great to be measured in words.

LEE DAVIS LODGE.

CONTENTS.

[1] The names of the characters in each play are retained throughout in their French forms.

A STUDY IN CORNEILLE.

CHAPTER I.

THE DEVELOPMENT OF THE FRENCH DRAMA.

IT is winter. Every flower has dropped its iris-tinted petals, the silvery music of the rills is hushed, over earth's frost-bound bosom is spread a spotless shroud, the trees of the forest stand like giant spectres manacled in ice, leaden clouds canopy the scene, all is dun and desolate and drear.

But nature, we know, is dead in appearance only. Soon the sun with lover's kiss shall bring once more the blushes to her cheek. Spring, crowned with violets, shall deck the fields in flower-embroidered robes of velvet green. The brook shall resume its merry warble as it wanders on its way. The birds shall make the leafy groves vocal with songs of praise. Above shall bend the skies of blue and

2

gold, and with revolving months shall come the abundant harvest of luscious fruit and yellow grain.

The Middle Ages were the winter of France. Deathful frosts of barbarism had long since nipped the efflorescence of classic genius. Deep lay the snows over all the land. But beneath their drifts were the germs of modern French philosophy, art and civilization.

Among other swelling seeds to be found in that cheerless period of preparation were the humble beginnings of the Drama. Upon these, even in the hasty sketch which is here attempted, we must bestow some passing glances. He who would understand any phenomenon, mental or material, must study it in the history of its evolution, in its genesis and growth. What, then, was the origin of the French Drama? It was the child of the church. The very power that had remorselessly crushed under her heel the pagan theatre—and rightly, too, for it had become the deadly foe both of religion and of morality—that same power was to bring forth the new drama, aye, and nourish it at her bosom.

Some scholars have indeed maintained, and not without a degree of probability, that the principles of Latin comedy were never utterly forgotten in Christendom. The art of Terence, it is contended, was not dead in the Middle Ages; it was only in a state of hibernation. In support of their position the advocates of this theory put in evidence such dramatic compositions as the six " comedies " written in Latin during the tenth century by Hrosvitha, the famous nun of Gandersheim. These plays, though ostensibly imitations of Terence and evincing considerable skill in the dramatic art, bear in form no marked resemblance to their model. They are written in prose pervaded by a certain rhythm, and interspersed with rhyme; their themes are taken from the legends of the saints; and it seems to have been the design of the authoress to shed a halo of glory about the sublimation of Christian character. Her dramas, composed, it is thought, for educational purposes, were read aloud or recited by the sisters of the convent. It is quite possible, indeed it is probable, that there were in France, also, such isolated examples of the survival, if we may call it so, of the ancient drama. But though it is doubtless true that here and there a learned priest or nun thus kept the flickering lamp of classicism burning in a lonely cell, the light was but feeble and fell not far beyond the precincts of the secluded cloister.

Another factor in the development of the early French drama was found in the strolling players, mimics and buffoons who, setting at naught the ban of the church and responding to the importunate demands of the populace for scenic representation, conserved in their peripatetic profession some of the traditions of the pagan stage.

Probably, also, the pilgrims who went into the Holy Land to do battle there for the cross against the crescent brought back with them to their native land some knowledge of dramatic composition and theatrical apparatus, acquired during their sojourn in the East. Besieged by admiring throngs eager to hear the thrilling adventures which had befallen them, these war-worn veterans, rich in honors but poor in purse, turned to account what they had learned of theatrical art, and acted before the spell-bound people, little dramas in which were repre-sented, first, perhaps, the high exploits of the cru-saders, and afterwards the stories of Holy Writ. Of course all the elements mentioned, the literary, the professional, and the pilgrim contributed to the growth of the drama. But the germ was furnished by the worship of the church.

So it was in Greece. The Hellenic theatre sprang from the worship of Dionysus, the special god of husbandmen, who was adored as the source of light, the ruler of the seasons and the divinity under whose benign dispensation the grape grew ruddy and the grain golden. All art, in fact, plants its roots deep down in the religious sentiment of man. At the high behest of religion, architecture arose to build the temples of the gods, sculpture to embody in marble man's highest conceptions of their divine forms, painting to illustrate their lives in pictured scene, music and poetry to waft to heaven on co-active wings the profoundest emotions of the soul.

We need not be surprised, then, to find the new drama implicit in the Roman Catholic liturgy which contained an epic element in the reading of the Scriptures by the priest and a lyric element in the answers and the anthems of the people. From these primordial forms by evolution and expansion came the mediaeval mysteries.

2*

On special occasions, in order to make the service more impressive and imposing, the Gospel story was illustrated by spectacular exhibitions and interspersed with song. Thus originated the liturgical mysteries. They were developed, beyond question, as early as the tenth century. In France, during the twelfth century certainly, if not, indeed, in the eleventh, short texts were composed in Latin for these religious dramas. Another degree of development was reached when, during the same period, they began to be written in the vernacular. Here we find the tap-root of mediaeval tragedy. So, also, the early comedy lies germinant in those burlesque dramas in which, at certain seasons of merry-making, the church allowed her children to indulge.

In her effort to excite the admiration and attract the affection of the rude, unlettered and simple-hearted people of the times, she had deigned to don both buskin and sock. Her worship she had in truth transformed into a gorgeous spectacle. The great Gothic cathedrals, with their clustered pillars, lofty spires, brilliantly colored windows, and exquisitely carved vaults, became so many mag-

nificent theatres.[1]   The church understood full
well that

> " Action is eloquence, and the eyes of the ignorant
>   More learned than their ears."

With what eager expectation did the people await
the recurrence of each great religious festival, when,
escaping for a time from under the dark wings of
the demon of care and laying aside their shields all
battered in the battle of life, they might feast their
eyes on sacred scenes, drink in long draughts of
music with ravished ear, and so satisfy at once the
cravings of the senses and the longings of the soul.
Imagine the emotions of the naïve spectators as they
saw represented before them the affecting stories of
the Holy Book.   At Christmastide the Babe of
Bethlehem was shown lying in the manger in the
midst of the oxen and receiving the adoration of the
shepherds and the wise men of the East.   A little
later the church with the strewing of palms com-

---

[1] It is by no means intended here to criticize adversely the
action of the church in permitting religious dramas.   On the
whole, her policy seems vindicated by the elevating effect upon
the (degraded) people of the times.

memorated his triumphal entry into Jerusalem. On Good Friday a veritable sepulchre stood ready to receive the crucified Lord of glory. At Easter, three men in snowy robes, wearing hoods on their heads, and holding in their hands silver flasks of consecrated oil, acted the rôle of the three women who came to the tomb at sunrise with sweet spices to anoint the Saviour; and a fourth man, also dressed in white, personated the angel who spake the glad words "HE IS RISEN." Thus it was that within the pale of the church the drama had been established.

The most ancient examples extant of the religious pieces are the dramatic liturgy of DANIEL, dating from the twelfth century and containing some passages in French; the mystery of Adam, belonging to the same century and written entirely in the vernacular; and the mystery of the Ten Virgins, a play which is of uncertain though, without doubt, very early date, and is composed part in Latin and part in French.

In the course of time the biblical narrative was embellished with touches of theatrical art and inlaid with the ornaments of invention. The legends of the saints, also, formed a rich mine of dramatic ore which was worked up betimes into miracle-plays. Of these the THÉOPHILE of Ruteboeuf, a *trouvère* who flourished in the thirteenth century, is an early sample. At length the drama was differentiated into independence. This epoch may be said to have arrived when, in the thirteenth century, Jean Bodel, of Arras, a *trouvère* who lived a joyous life of gayety and song until leprosy laid its loathsome touch upon him, published his "JEU DE SAINT NICOLAS," a miracle-play, written in French alone, and based upon two earlier pieces on the same subject, both of which had been represented in the churches for a great many years. One of these pieces, a dialogue composed in Latin rhyme with refrains in the *Langue d'Oïl*, had been produced during the eleventh century by Hilarius, a disciple of Abelard; the other piece, of later date, was the work of a monk of S. Bénoit-sur-Loire and was written in Latin. To Bodel belongs the honor of giving form and fashion to the serious drama. His play, though it had been evolved from the offices of the church and though the weight of its moral was cast on the side of Christianity, is so far from being hampered by the trammels of the church's tutelage that the best scenes in the piece derive their color and tone from tavern life. As the character of this drama was probably too secular to permit its being acted in the church, the representation took place most likely either in the public square of Arras, or in the spacious hall of some rich citizen's dwelling. Thus did the theatre attain its majority. Henceforth the church will regard its offspring with but a fickle fondness, now smiling at filial duty, now frowning on sturdy independence.

What Bodel did for the serious drama, another native of Arras living in the thirteenth century, Adam de la Halle, well known, also, in the history of French letters as Adam le Bossu and Le Bossu d'Arras, did for comedy. No reason can now be discovered why he should have been given this nickname. He himself denies any such deformity in these explicit words : " *On m'apele bochu, mès je ne le sui mie.*" After spending his early years at the abbey of Vaucelles, sur l'Escant near Cambray, Adam returned to the paternal roof. Soon he fell in love with a young woman whom he married only to abandon at the first onset of the cares of housekeeping. Not content with thus deserting his wife, he afterward made her the butt of jests upon the stage. His first poems were sweet with sentiment; his later ones acrid with satire. The most important of his works are the "JEU DE LA FEUILLIE," a farce in which he portrays with piquant pen his domestic infelicities, and the "JEU DE ROBIN ET MARION," a dramatized pastorelle. In the former piece we have the first fruits of comedy; the latter is the first comic opera.

Jean Bodel and Adam de la Halle, the two men who had thus led the drama forth from the sanctuary and far afield, were the foster-fathers of the French theatre. Until long after these writers had gone to their graves, however, the mysteries, which, properly speaking, were adaptations of the scriptural narrative, and the miracle-plays which embodied the wondrous stories of the saints, continued to be the staples of the stage. All the sections of the Old and the New Testaments containing a dramatic element were recast into mysteries, and put upon the boards. With rapt attention the people, whose minds were untainted by the *nil admirari* sentiment of civilized shallowness or by unthinking or surface-

thinking infidelity, and whose hearts throbbed and
thrilled with the great problems of duty and of
destiny, gazed with the liveliest emotions of pity and
terror upon spectacles in which were represented life
and death, resurrection and judgment, heaven and
hell.   The most interesting of these mysteries,
whether we regard its historical importance, the
sublimity of the subject, the magnificence of the
scenic decorations, or the literary skill displayed,
is "THE MYSTERY OF THE PASSION."   This drama
which depicted the whole life of our Lord and
required several days for its representation, embraced
eighty-seven characters, including the three persons
of the Trinity, six angels, six devils, twelve apostles,
Herod and his court and Pilate and his soldiers.
The stage must have been a queer sight.   It con-
sisted of scaffolding rising tier upon tier, sometimes
to the height of nine stories.   The highest story
which represented Paradise had a gilt balustrade and
contained the "CHAIRE PARÉE" of the Deity.   The
lowest story exhibited the hideous horrors of hell.
In the intermediate stories were shown the various
rooms, temples or places in which the events had
occurred.   This mystery, with others, was acted by

a society made up of citizens of Paris, locksmiths, master-masons and the like, who under the name of Confraternity of the Passion and Resurrection of our Lord, were authorized on December 4, 1402, by letters patent from Charles VI to represent their dramas at any suitable place in Paris or its suburbs. Extreme realism distinguished the acting. Whenever a character was to be belabored in the play with fists, or lash, or club, real blows were rained upon him with a vigorous earnestness designed to excite the mirth of the spectators. Fighting and killing were often represented with a fidelity which lacked but little of the grim reality. The gay and the grave, the ribald and the reverent, here jostled each other, and comical devils drew shouts of laughter from assemblies who were soon to weep over the Saviour's tragic death.

The mysteries, which were sometimes forty or even fifty thousand lines in length, often required several days for their representation, and were, therefore, divided not into acts but into *journées*, or days, a term afterward employed for acts by the Spanish dramatists. Toward these plays the attitude of the church was very friendly, priests as well as people thronging

3

to see them.   So similar to the mysteries in general character were the miracle-plays that they need no separate description here.

Another variety of drama of later origin is found in the MORALITIES, a class of plays which mark the advance of the public mind from childlike faith to active reason, and in which the characters represented are the Virtues and the Vices personified. Though they sprang from the mysteries, the moralities undoubtedly owed their peculiar form to that universal craze for allegory among the French which found its ideal and its idol in the "ROMAN DE LA ROSE," and which was for the two centuries following the composition of that famous poem the preeminent and predominant factor in poetic style.

I select one of these dramas as a specimen.   BANQUET invites to his lavish board EAT-ALL, THIRST, I-DRINK-TO-YOU and SANS-WATER, all merry companions.   The ladies DAINTINESS, GLUTTONY and LUST complete the party.   A rich feast is served, the guests partake freely of the good cheer, and all is revelry.   But suddenly bursting in upon the scene COLIC, GOUT, JAUNDICE, QUINSY and DROPSY seize in their clutches the hilarious guests, some of whom are overcome, while others seek aid from SOBRIETY. The latter requests CURE to assist him. BANQUET is tried before JUDGE EXPERIENCE, convicted and condemned to be hung. DIET executes the sentence.

Two thousand lines may be considered the average length of a morality, though some of them very greatly exceeded that limit. They were acted by a guild consisting of members of the legal profession called the CLERKS OF THE BASOCHE or PALACE OF JUSTICE whom Philip the Fair had established about 1303 as a regular corporation, and upon whom he had bestowed certain privileges, among others that of giving theatrical representations. From such allegorical pieces as the moralities the transition to the FARCE was easy. The popularity of the serious drama was on the wane. Amusement instead of devotion or instruction in the faith was becoming more and more the object of those who frequented the theatre. The people craved plays filled with fun and folly.

Then there came to enrich with treasures of wit the still scant thesaurus of comedy, this autochthonic species of drama, the farce, which was instinct with the ESPRIT GAULOIS, and whose embryon had been carried inchoate within the fecund fabliau. In these jocular plays, which were about five hundred lines long, many phases of life were mirrored. Connubial infelicities, the failings of women, the faults and foibles of the clergy, the shifts of social parasites, the pretensions of pedantry, and the like, were all marks for the arrows of the dramatist's mischievous, not to say malicious, wit.

The AVOCAT PATHELIN, a farce supposed to belong to the middle or to the earlier part of the fifteenth century, published in 1490, and containing the famous quotation, "REVENONS À NOS MOUTONS," holds the highest rank, not only among pieces of this genre, but also among the dramas of the mediaeval French stage.

Last in the line of development, and partaking of the nature both of the morality and of the farce, arose the SOTIE, a kind of political comedy in which abuses of all sorts in church and state, in public life and private life, were attacked with the scorpion lash of satire. The soties, containing usually, like the farces, about five hundred lines, were composed and played by a company of well born young Parisians, styled the ENFANTS SANS SOUCI, whose leader was called LE PRINCE DES SOTS, and wore a hood adorned with ass's ears. Some of the advertisements in which these jolly actors solicited public patronage were droll enough. The following may be taken as a sample:

> "Sotz lunatiques, sotz estourdis, sotz sages,
> Sotz de villes, de chasteaux, de villages,
> Sotz rassotés, sotz nyais, sotz subtilz,
> Sotz amoureux, sotz privés, sotz sauvages,
> Sotz vieux, nouveaux, et sotz de toutes âges,
> Sotz barbares, estrangers et gentilz,
> Sotz raisonnables, sotz pervers, sotz restifz,
> Vostre prince, sans nulles intervalles,
> Le mardi gras, jouera ses jeux aux Halles."

The unbridled license of the ENFANTS SANS SOUCI, who spared no man whether he wore coronet or cowl, nay who had even dared to turn upon both prince and pope, at length caused Francis I to put his royal veto upon soties and farces. Well might the king fear plays so menacing to the public peace. In 1548 the Parliament of Paris influenced by the inrushing tide of the Reformation also interdicted the mysteries on the ground that they were indecent and profane.

3*

Thus did both the secular and the sacred drama of that period receive an " *immedicabile vulnus*," for, though the CONFRATERNITY OF THE PASSION, who subsequently came to be called COMEDIANS OF THE HÔTEL DE BOURGOGNE, were permitted for long after 1548 to act farces instead of the mysteries in Paris, and though the latter plays still lingered on in the provinces, yet the glory of the mediaeval theatre then was gone, and the days of its dominance were numbered.

In this brief account of the early French drama I have not attempted to draw the complete curve of its evolution. My task has been much lighter. I have only tried to locate the cardinal points through which the curve passed. More than one critic has regretted that a drama so truly national in its nature should have perished thus in the freshness of its prime, instead of attaining, like the Spanish and the English drama, to a full and splendid development. Such laments are idle now, however. It is possible, indeed, that, had this mediæval drama continued, some poet Titan, some French Shakspere with many-sided soul would have arisen in the fulness of time to transmute by the wonderful alchemy of his genius all that was base into finest gold. But we must leave such speculation to the apostles of the phantom philosophy of the might have been. Ours the duty now to herald the advent of another and a very different school of dramatic literature.

The resplendent orb of literary genius which once had shed such radiant glory over Greece had, indeed, sunk below the sapphire waves of the classic sea. But preceded by a van-guard of lesser lights, and shining with a lustre borrowed from that generous orb, another luminary arose above the horizon of France to pour a silver sheen o'er all her lovely hills and dales.

The times were propitious for the resurrection of classic form and the revival of classic spirit. The one hundred years from 1450 to 1550 constitute one of the most momentous epochs in the history of man. Civilization in seven-leagued boots was stepping then from peak to peak of progress. The dauntless Columbus conquered the sea, and, while about the anchored ships the Oceanides were weeping for their father's broken sceptre, unfurled the banner of Castile in a new world, fairer far than the Atlantis of tradition. Feudalism, whose breastplate had been shattered by powder and ball, was tottering to its death. Consolidated, centralized monarchies, girt and guarded by standing armies in serried files, were being firmly established. The genius of the classic lands had risen from the tomb of time, and stood pointing out the path of glory to modern scholars. Printing gave wings to the immortal words of the ancient masters. Copernicus, looking through the roof of his humble farmhouse and seeing the planets in choral dance go tripping round their central sun, demolished the hoary Ptolemaic theory of the heavens. Last in the list we may mention the great religious revolution led by Luther, which stirred men's souls to their depths and finally filled all Europe with the din and dust of battle. Thus while the channel of thought was being wonderfully broadened and deepened, its volume and velocity were being correspondingly increased. It is with the revival of learning, however, that we are particularly concerned here. This had begun, indeed, long before the period of which we have just spoken.

In the early part of the fifteenth century Italian scholars had devoted themselves with passionate love to the study of Greek and Roman letters. The famous books on which the dust of ages long had lain spoke once more in mellow tones their manifold messages to mankind. The greatest enthusiasm for classical culture took possession of all. On the fall of Constantinople, therefore, in 1453, Italy welcomed with open arms the Greek scholars who had been compelled to flee to her from that city bringing with them the Greek language, learning and literature, gems more precious far than all the storied riches of the East. With what lively joy, with what tender affection were those heirlooms of the ages received by Italian scholars.

The deeper they drank at the limpid fountain of antiquity, the greater grew their reverence and admiration. The effects of the new culture upon polite society were marvellous. Soon the whole lump was fermented by the classic leaven. Oft times this love for the glorious past ran into excess. Thus it happened in Italy, as afterward in other countries, that the RENAISSANCE, instead of simply performing its proper function of enlightening the intellect, purifying the taste and quickening the imagination, not seldom led to servile imitation which stunted growth

and repressed originality. Thus, also, in the later
history of the movement HUMANISM was destined
to degenerate into PAGANISM. These, however, were
but abuses of the legacy left by antiquity.

From Italy the potent influence of the revival of
learning, borne first in the chariot of war, passed
northward into France. Here were seen the same
results. The classical humanities percolated through
all the strata of literary life. The grey-haired scholar,
going back to the school-room, and not then "creep-
ing like snail, unwillingly," pored over the glowing
pages of the Greek and Roman authors. Royalty
stretched above arts and letters its protecting aegis.
The fashions and usages of society were tinged with
a classical hue. The antique costumes of Athens
and Rome became *à la mode* in Paris. On all sides
the past was idolized. The climax of affected classicism was reached when pedants, patterning after
Plutarch's heroes, even died declaiming in ambitious
rhetoric.

To us all these transports seem very extravagant.
But let us try to put ourselves in the places of the
men of that time. Coming forth once more into
the light after long centuries of weary wandering

in that midnight forest, the Middle Ages, the human
race suddenly beheld in raptured vision all the greatness and the glory of antiquity.

"L'Europe moderne," says M. Michelet in that
vivid style of his, "L'Europe moderne revoyait sa
mère, l'antiquité, et se jetait dans ses bras. L'Orient
va se rapprocher tout à l'heure, tout à l'heure l'Améri-
que. Spectacle digne de l'œil de Dieu! La famille
humaine réunie, à travers les lieux et les temps, se
regardant, se retrouvant, pleurant de s'être méconnue.
Combien cette grande mère, la noble, la sereine, l'hé-
roïque antiquité, parut supérieure à tout ce qu'on con-
naissait, quand on revit, après tant de siècles, sa face
vénérable et charmante! 'O mère! que vous êtes
jeune!' disait le monde avec des larmes, 'de quels
attraits imposants nous vous revoyons parée! Vous
emportâtes au tombeau la ceinture éternellement ra-
jeunissante de la mère d'amour.—Et moi, pour un
millier d'années, me voici tout courbé et déjà sous
les rides.'"

As they are admitted into the Voltaic circuit of
classic civilization—a circuit whose poles are Athens
and Rome—an electric thrill runs through the souls
of all scholars in this age of transition. Ancient

inspiration weds modern aspiration. In the still-
ness of the study these eager disciples of the past
hear from afar the melodious accents of the poet and
the rhythmic roll of the orator's periods, sounding
and resounding down the corridors of time. The
prophets of the new culture are ravished with delight.
They are carried back on the wings of imagination
to that beautiful land whither in the roseate dawn
of European civilization while the dew was on the
lilies and the lark was in the skies poetry came from
heaven to live on earth with men—to the birth-place
of philosophy and domicile of art—to the purple
hills and flower-starred vales of Greece,

> "Where each old poetic mountain,
>   Inspiration breathed around;
>   Every shade and hallowed fountain
>   Murmured deep a solemn sound."

Each scholar inhales the air of Helicon, sails on
the foam-fringed billows of the Aegean, and visits
with a pilgrim's devotion every famous spot. It is
his priceless privilege to converse and commune with
some of the mightiest masters that ever swayed and
sculptured the minds of men. The martial strains

of Homer fire his soul; the sublime creations of Aeschylus fill him with awe; the matchless genius of Sophocles compels the homage of his heart; he weeps with Euripides and laughs with Aristophanes; he listens now to the artless prattle of Herodotus and now to the profound disquisitions and forceful phrase of Thucydides; he hears from the bema the burning words of " the famous orators,"

> " whose resistless eloquence
> Wielded at will that fierce democratie,
> Shook the arsenal and fulmined over Greece
> To Macedon and Artaxerxes' throne;"

with sympathetic sigh he joins the little circle that in the cell of Socrates are holding their last colloquy with the great philosopher while the lengthening shadows fall about them, and the sun slowly sinks to his couch of crimson cloud; in the groves of the old Academy he walks and talks with the divine Plato; he hoards as gems in memory's casket the wisdom-weighted words of the Stagirite.

Then as he turns away from " the city of the violet crown," with his heart full of sadness for her fallen glory, Rome, " the land of scholars and the

4

nurse of arms," she who caught from the dying lips
of Greece the divine afflatus of genius, also claims
from him an honorable meed for a long array of
warriors and statesmen, orators and poets, philosophers and historians. And well may the imperial
mistress of the world challenge his admiration, for
Cicero's impassioned bursts of eloquence are hers
and the liquid lines of Vergil—hers the sententious
verse of Horace, the fertile fancy of Ovid and the
brilliant colors of Livy—hers the "*ingenium facile
et copiosum*" of Seneca, the scorching scorn of
Juvenal and the moral dignity of Tacitus. Right
royal fellowship is this that is offered here.

What wonder that, being thus put into closest
relations with the intellectual life of both Greece
and Rome, being thus nourished, as it were, upon
the powerful elixir of ancient culture, the French
scholars of the sixteenth century should feel as if
they had indeed experienced a renaissance, a re-birth,
a re-creation? What wonder that when the majestic
rhythm of the two classic cantos in the poem of
man's earthly life was ringing in their ears, and
when the superb beauty of the classic languages and
the unrivalled splendor of the classic literatures

were ever before their eyes, the enthusiastic students of the past should try to trick out in borrowed ornaments the comparatively homely speech of France, and to supersede the native varieties in French letters by exotics from Greece and Rome?

In this era of imitation, which was ushered in by Pierre Ronsard [1524–1585], arose the classical drama—a drama born to immortality, though destined, as will be seen, to display during its early history far more of the traits of Seneca, Plautus and Terence than of that noble Greek art whose glorious productions those writers were well content to copy.

Étienne Jodelle, one of the sailing-stars in Ronsard's Pléiade, was the pioneer playwright of the new school. In 1552 he gave to the public his CLÉOPÂTRE CAPTIVE, a meagre tragedy, modelled after the style of Seneca, furnished with a chorus, and written in iambic decasyllables and Alexandrines. This play, however barren in incident and dull in interest it may seem to our eyes, was yet the prophecy and pledge of the great Corneille. The other pieces of Jodelle were LA RENCONTRE and EUGÈNE, comedies, and DIDON, a tragedy. Eugène, a licentious attack upon the vices of the rich clergy, is esteemed his best effort.

The next noticeable name after Jodelle is Jacques Grévin, a Calvinistic physician. His tragedy, LA MORT DE CÉSAR, contains according to La Harpe "grand and beautiful ideas and the real tone of tragedy." Grévin composed two comedies, also, LES ESHABIS and LA TRÉSORIÈRE, which, like the most of those written in the sixteenth century, were disfigured by gross licentiousness.

But the two authors who brought the classical tragedy to its highest elevation before Corneille were Robert Garnier [1545–1601] and Antoine de Montchrestien [d. 1621]. Garnier wrote eight tragedies. The best of these is the biblical play, LES JUIVES. Euripides and Seneca were the masters from whom Garnier learned his craft. Seneca especially he closely imitated. His work is marred by the faults which were then found in almost all the dramas of the kind introduced by Jodelle, lack of action, paucity of characters and interminable speeches. Messengers by opportune recitals carry forward the story, the chorus is retained and in BRADAMANTE, a tragic comedy whose plot is taken from Ariosto, Garnier for the first time in the history of the French drama brings upon the stage that ill-starred, insipid personage, the confidant. Yet this author's style is not without dignity, nor his versification without harmony, and his plays are often adorned with noble sentiments. He paints the passions, also, with something closely akin to power. Upon the whole Ronsard's tribute is not greatly exaggerated :

> "Par toi, Garnier, la scène des François,
> Se change en or qui n'étoit que de bois."

Antoine de Montchrestien wrote six tragedies, the best of which is L'Écossaise. His chief merits are his effective rhetoric, his improvement over his predecessors in the delineation of character, the beauty of his choric odes, and the superior elegance of his versification.

A high rank must also be awarded in the literary history of this epoch to Pierre Larivey [1540–1610–1620], an Italian by birth who settled in France. Larivey [L'arrivé] is simply a translation of his real name Giunto. He wrote twelve comedies in prose. These were all copied from Italian proto-

4*

types which in turn were themselves often imitations of Plautus and Terence. Yet Larivey was no mere echo. He was a man of real talent. Copy his plays he might, but he always threw into their composition something original, something " *de lui et à lui.*"

In dramatic skill Garnier himself is, perhaps, inferior to him. Certain it is that his plays, which are especially distinguished for the vivacity of their dialogue, constitute a stage in the evolution of French comedy.

Alexandre Hardy [1560–1631], a master of scenic effect and a man of extraordinary fertility, was far less classical, but far more natural, and therefore far more national, than his predecessors. While adopting the general scheme of the classical tragedy and usually observing the unity of action, he repudiates the restrictions as to place and time. " Hardy was irregular enough," says Guizot, " to have been a Shakspere, if he had possessed a Shakspere's genius." But no such genius had fallen to Hardy's lot. Nevertheless his plays, in which action, character and life abound, sometimes exhibit considerable power. He was a great plagiarist. The authors of Spain especially he despoiled without scruple.

THE FRENCH DRAMA. 39

Different authorities variously state the number of his plays at from five to seven hundred, of which forty-one are extant. Perhaps the inferior quality of his work is partly due to the fact that his wings were pinioned by poverty. Sometimes in his hard struggle to get bread for himself and his troop of actors, he had to compose as many as two thousand lines in twenty-four hours. And yet, despite his native defects and all the disadvantages of his environment, his was the great honor of giving some useful hints to the budding genius of Corneille.

Of the numerous other dramatic writers who immediately preceded that immortal master on the stage, we shall mention only three, Théophile de Viaud, Jean Mairet and Jean Rotrou. Viaud [1590–1626] is noticeable for his tragedy "PYRAME ET THISBE," which, though deformed by such wretched conceits as were common to the *estilo culto* of Spain and to the ridiculous imitation of that style then fashionable in France, sometimes displays an elegance far above anything in Hardy.

Jean Mairet [1604–1686] made his début as a dramatic author when he was about sixteen years old. His only piece of real value, however, is

"SOPHONISBE," a tragedy planned in obedience to the precepts of Aristotle, and the date of whose appearance is variously given as 1629 and 1633.

Rotrou [1609–1660], who produced his first play, a tragi-comedy, entitled "L'HYPOCONDRIAQUE OU LE MORT AMOUREUX," in 1628, one year before the appearance of Corneille's "MÉLITE," was a man worthy to associate even with such a prince among poets. Rotrou's next piece was "LA BAGUE DE L'OUBLI," a comedy which also came out in 1628. Subsequently to the performance of "MÉLITE," he wrote many other dramas. But the two plays upon which his fame rests, "LE VÉRITABLE SAINT GENESTE" [1646] and "VENCESLAS" [1647] were not composed until his friend Corneille had given to France his early masterpieces, each of which was to be κτῆμα εἰς ἀεί. We may, therefore, dismiss Rotrou for the present, reserving for a future work an account of his character and genius.

Here we must close our very imperfect sketch of the theatre from Jodelle to Corneille. As yet dramatic art is only a potential and the drama itself a mere admixture, consisting of rude imitation of classic form and a large infusion of Spanish grandiosity, grandiloquence and stage-tricks, together with a liberal amount of Italian affectation. Good taste in the period just before Corneille was a thing utterly unknown among both the playwrights and the public. However slovenly might be a dramatist's style, however much rodomontade there might be in his declamation or euphuism in his dialogue, if he kept up the interest of the spectators by a lavish use of romance, if he scattered with free hand such fascinating charms as abductions and infidelities, prisons and police, disguises and discoveries, poisons and duels through his pieces, he was pretty certain to obtain the applause of his audience. He was not forced to lie upon the Procrustean bed of ancient drama, but might give full play to all the extravagance of his imagination.

The despotism of the three unities had not then been generally established. Their authority, while upheld by some, was disregarded by many others. Nowhere was there a clarified concept of order, proportion and fitness. The stage was occupied by plays full of movement, indeed, but monstrous in construction, bombastic in style, devoid of real passion, often indecent, abounding in whimsical conceits, but smacking little of Attic salt.

"Quel désordre!" exclaims Racine, looking backward upon the theatre of that time, "quelle irrégularité! nul goût, nulle connaissance des véritables beautés du théâtre; les auteurs aussi ignorants que les spectateurs; la plupart des sujets extravagants et dénués de vraisemblance; point de moeurs, point de caractères; la diction encore plus vicieuse que l'action et dont les pointes et de misérables jeux de mots faisaient le principal ornement; en un mot, toutes les règles de l'art, celles même de l'honnêteté et de la bienséance partout violées."

All was thus confusion. In its chaotic condition the drama may without much inaccuracy be described in the words of Ovid, as

"rudis indigestaque moles,
Nec quicquam, nisi pondus iners, congestaque eodem
Non bene junctarum discordia semina rerum."

Then came "ille opifex" with law and light and life; then came PIERRE CORNEILLE to fashion with creative touch the true classical drama of France.

CHAPTER II.

The Formative Period in Corneille's Career.

THE seventeenth century in France was one of those ganglionic epochs which originate the nervous force in the organism of history.

Six other eras in six other countries may be mentioned as similarly vital and vivific in the chronicles of European culture. These eras are, first, the golden age of Greek art, literature and philosophy, a period extending from the battle of Salamis through the resplendent administration of Pericles down to the death of Aristotle; second, the epoch made glorious in Roman annals not less by the literary genius of Cicero and Sallust, of Vergil and Horace, of Livy and Ovid, than by the mighty achievements of Cæsar and Augustus; third, modern Italy's proudest period, the age of Lorenzo de Medici and of the great artists, Leonardo da Vinci, Raphael and Michelangelo;

fourth, that famous era in Spanish literature, when
Cervantes, Lope de Vega and Calderon adorned
their native land with their brilliant productions;
fifth, the age of Elizabeth and James which was
transfigured by the dazzling effulgence of Spenser,
Hooker, Shakspere and Bacon; sixth and last, the
formative and determinative period in the literary
history of Germany when her gifted sons Klopstock,
Lessing, Kant, Goethe and Schiller caused her name
to be sounded by the trumpet-tones of fame everywhere throughout the world of letters.

France, in the early years of the seventeenth century, was enjoying an unwonted degree of peace,
order and prosperity. Upon the throne sat Henry
IV, the white-plumed hero of Ivry. His was a
reign of wisdom. By the edict of Nantes (April
13, 1598) which secured to the Huguenots religious
liberty and civil justice, he put a stop to intestine
strife; by the treaty of Vervins with Spain (May 2,
1598) he concluded on terms honorable to himself
the war with that country; by an enlightened domestic administration, conducted under his authority by
his sagacious minister Sully, who brought the provinces more directly and completely under the king's

control, made extensive internal improvements and thoroughly reorganized the system of finances, he greatly advanced the material welfare of his people.

Thus the ship of state was fairly launched upon a strong and steady tide to wealth and glory. But on May 14, 1610, Henry was stabbed to death by the dagger of a fanatic, François Ravaillac. The tears of all France fell thick and fast upon the good king's grave.

Marie de Medici, widow of Henry and mother of Louis XIII, who was only nine years old when his father died, now became regent. By nature at once passionate and weak, she was easily manipulated as a tool by her Italian favorites. Her regency was characterized by deplorable disorders, reckless expenditure of public money, and, in short, by all the abuses of absolutism, without any of those redeeming traits of benevolence and beneficence which have sometimes made absolutism in some sort bearable.

Her prime minister, Concino de Concini, Maréchal et Marquis d'Ancre, was heartily hated by the people as an insolent upstart. Over the young king, whom his presumptuous manner naturally nettled, he exercised a species of guardianship which became

5

well-nigh a custody. From this odious restraint Louis was freed April 24, 1617, when with his approval Maréchal d'Ancre was assassinated in the Louvre.

The king, thus by murder made master of the situation, now took the reins of government into his own hands. He committed to his favorite, Albert de Luynes, the affairs of state. Marie de Medici retired to Blois. A period of confusion ensued. After some resistance, not worthy to be dignified by the name of war, the queen-mother submitted to her son, and a treaty was made between them, August 10, 1620.

The career of de Luynes was cut short by death from a malignant fever on December 17, 1621. Not a few strove to clamber up into the place and power that had once been his.

But a man was now about to step forward into prominence who, thrusting France into the fires of his genius, was then with mighty strokes to shape the glowing mass anew upon his ringing anvil. This man was Cardinal Richelieu. He was made a member of the king's council in 1624. August prelate, profound statesman, astute politician, crafty intriguer, Maecenas of letters—all these titles belong to Richelieu. Keeping his eye ever steadily fixed upon his great aims and little scrupulous as to the means which he employed to attain them, he made himself all-powerful at home, and France a queen among nations.

Louis XIII was quite a secondary figure. His only claim, indeed, to the praise of history is that he was wise enough, although inwardly disliking Richelieu, still to accept him as a guide in the perplexities of politics.

The policy of Richelieu may be summed up under two heads: first, he strove by humbling the high nobility and by destroying the political power of the Huguenots to make the authority of the royal government absolutely supreme in the land; second, he strained every nerve to humiliate the house of Austria, and so exalt France in the eyes of Europe. While the great Cardinal was thus laying the granite foundations of his country's future glory, Pierre Corneille arose to fulfil his grand mission in literature.

The illustrious dramatist was born at Rouen, June 6, 1606. His father, who was also named

Pierre Corneille, was royal advocate at the marble table of Normandy and master of waters and forests in the viscounty of Rouen. He was a faithful and fearless official, as is abundantly proved by the very laudatory *lettres de noblesse* granted him by Louis XIII in January, 1637, a distinction rendered doubly significant from the fact that in January, 1634, the king had announced in an edict " that for the future he would not grant any letters to confer nobility, except for great and important considerations."

The poet's mother, Marthe, was a Le Pesant de Boisguilbert, a distinguished name in that locality. Her father was a *Maître des Comptes*. Corneille came thus of honorable lineage on both sides. As his was a family of lawyers, he was designed for the bar, and was educated for that profession at the Jesuits' College in Rouen, where he won a prize in 1618 or 1619.

But the forum was not to be the scene of his glory. While he was at college in Rouen, he fell in love, so he tells us, with a little girl who afterward became Mme. de Pont, wife of a *Maître des Comptes* of that place. This early affection flowered into poetry. So love first led the poet Corneille within the sacred precincts of Parnassus.

But, though he himself says:

> "Charmé de deux beaux yeux, mon vers charma la cour
> Et ce que j'ai de mieux, je le dois à l'amour,"

it is altogether improbable that he owed his fame in any proper sense to the inspiration of the tender passion of his youth. In another place he states with probably much greater accuracy the part that love had played in making him a poet:

> "Soleils, flambeaux, attraits, appas,
> Pleurs, désespoir, tourments, trépas,
> Tout ce petit meuble de bouche
> Dont un amoureux s'escarmouche
> Je savais bien m'en escrimer;
> Par là je m'appris à rimer."

I thereby learned to rhyme. That is about the truth of the matter.

Fontenelle, the nephew of Corneille, has, indeed, assigned to love a more important influence upon the development of his genius. After mentioning that the young Corneille first appeared at the

5*

bar "sans goût et sans succès," Fontenelle continues thus :

"But a small occasion disclosed in him a genius altogether different; and it was love that gave rise to the incident. A young man among his friends, in love with a young lady of the same city, took him to her house. The newcomer rendered himself more agreeable than the introducer. The pleasure of this occurrence awakened in M. Corneille a talent of which he was unconscious; and upon this light subject he composed the comedy of Mélite, which appeared in 1625. In it was discovered an original character, it was surmised that comedy was going to be perfected, and upon the confidence felt in the new author who was coming into notice there was formed a new troop of comedians."

It is really too bad to spoil this pleasant little anecdote, but the evidence seems to be against it. The comedy of Mélite, whose date the best authorities fix not as 1625 but as 1629, starts out, it is true, with such an incident. There is no ground, however, for supposing this to be a bit of autobiography. Corneille, as we have seen, had already, while still a collegian, been pierced by one of Cupid's golden arrows. Nor was the attachment a fleeting one, for in 1635 or 1636 the poet, writing about his little sweetheart of early days, declares :

> " Je ne vois rien d'aimable après l'avoir aimée ;
> Aussi n'aimai-je plus, et nul objet vainqueur
> N'a possédé depuis ma veine ni mon coeur."

From this emphatic statement it appears that Corneille's first love had been up to this date his only love. Now these two attachments, the love of Corneille, the student, for a little girl—a love which was not for many years followed by another—and the love, mentioned by Fontenelle, of Corneille, the full-fledged lawyer, for a young lady in society, are surely incompatible. We must, therefore, I think, give up, however reluctantly, this well-known story about the origin of Mélite.

To that comedy we now turn. The reader who expects to find here some earnest of Corneille's after greatness will be grievously disappointed. While it is decidedly superior to the pieces then in vogue, Mélite is still, when judged absolutely by any just standard, a very poor play, illuminated by no coruscations of genius, and marred by many blemishes of taste.

In beginning his examination of the firstling of his brain, Corneille says :

" This piece was my first essay, and it makes no attempt at conforming to the rules, for I did not then know that there were any. I had no guide but a little common sense, together with the examples of the late M. Hardy, whose vein was fertile rather than polished, and of a few moderns who were beginning to appear, and who were not more regular than he. Its success was surprising : it established a new troop of comedians at Paris, in spite of the merit of that which was in the sole possession of the stage there ; it equalled everything most beautiful that had been done up to that time, and made me known at court. This common sense which was all my rule, had made me hit upon the unity of action to set four lovers at variance by a single intrigue, and had given me enough aversion for that horrible irregularity which put Paris, Rome and Constantinople upon the same stage, to cause me to reduce mine to a single city."

As yet, however, the poet saw through a glass darkly. The plot of Mélite is simple enough. The play, which extends over more than a month, opens

with a conversation between Éraste and his friend
Tircis. Éraste who cherishes a fervent love for
Mélite laments her coldness to him. Tircis at first
discredits his friend's statement. When Éraste insists that it is too true, Tircis declares it a matter of
no great importance, anyhow, since his friend surely
can have no intention of marrying Mélite. But that,
Éraste protests, is just what he does intend to do, and
he breaks into high-flown praises of her charms :

"The day that she was born," he exclaims, "Venus, although
immortal,
Thought she would die of shame at seeing her so beautiful,
The Graces in emulation of one another descended from the
heavens,
In order to give themselves the honor of accompanying her eyes;
Love, who could not enter into her heart,
Wished obstinately to dwell upon her face."

To this affected speech, Tircis replies that such
sentiment soon evaporates after marriage. Moreover he thinks that

"Marriage of itself is such a heavy burden,
That one should dread it as much as the grave,"

Éraste, believing that Tircis will change his opinion when he sees Mélite, offers to introduce him to

her in order to test the matter. The invitation is accepted, and the two friends repair to the residence of Mélite, where her beauty achieves an easy victory over the indifference of Tircis.

In the course of the conversation which takes place between the trio, some further examples of the unnatural style of the times occur. When Tircis, speaking to Mélite, refers to the love which she kindles in men's hearts, she answers :

> " I do not receive love and I do not give any to anybody,
> How could I give whát I never had? "

Soon after she says to the plaintive Éraste :

> " to put an end to your woes and your passion
> Borrow all at once the coldness of my soul."

Éraste replies :

> " When I see you coldness loses all its power ;
> And you only preserve it because you do not see yourself."

> "Ah ! what ! " cries Mélite, " have all the mirrors false glasses ? "

All this is truly harrowing. However, we must proceed. After the interview with Mélite, although he solemnly assures his friend to the contrary,

Tircis secretly forms a firm resolution to win her love at all hazards.

Then comes a scene between Cloris, the sister of Tircis, and her lover Philandre, from which I extract the following saccharine conceits. Philandre has just asked Cloris whether she thinks herself much more lovable than he is:

Cloris.

Without doubt; and what couldst thou have that might be comparable to me?

Philandre.

Look into my eyes, and recognize that in me
One can see something as perfect as thou art.

Cloris.

That is without difficulty, seeing myself there reflected.

Philandre.

Turn from that vain picture by which thy sight is charmed.
Thou seest there only my heart, which has no longer a single feature
Save those that it has received from thy charming portrait,
And which, just as soon as thou didst appear,
In order to see thee better, took its place at the window.

Now for the intrigue which sets four lovers at variance. Éraste, convinced of the treachery of Tircis, and thirsting for revenge, sends to Philandre some fictitious love-letters purporting to come from Mélite, and containing flattering avowals of an irrepressible affection. The absurd vanity and credulity displayed by Philandre at this turn of affairs constitute a glaring defect in the play. Though he has never spoken to Mélite and does not know her handwriting, he accepts the letters as genuine and basely deserts his fiancée.

He does not visit Mélite, however, because he has been requested in this bogus correspondence not to do so until she shall have succeeded in clearing the coast of his rivals. At length, so a letter says, Tircis alone remains to be dismissed. When he, joyful in the assurance of Mélite's affection, confides his good fortune to Philandre, that poor dupe shows him the fraudulent letters. Here occurs another unpardonable defect. Tircis, in spite of the explicit declarations which he has received from Mélite's own mouth, and in spite of the fact that he, like Philandre, is entirely unacquainted with her chirography, yields immediately a foolish credence to the letters without seeking any explanation, and becomes almost frenzied with rage and grief.

In the first heat of his wrath, Tircis challenges Philandre to mortal combat. Philandre, however, who does not seem to be over brave, will not fight, or at least not until he shall have obtained Mélite's permission. Afterwards, indeed, he changes his mind, and goes hunting for his opponent, but fails to find him.

Tircis shows to Cloris the letters which he has gotten from Philandre, and which sufficiently explain the state of affairs. She, gay-hearted girl that she is, takes her lover's perfidy very philosophically, and, repairing to the home of Mélite, confronts her with the letters. Mélite, of course, repudiates them as spurious. Cloris, however, will credit no denial.

While the two girls are holding their colloquy, Lisis, a friend of Tircis, in order to put Mélite's fidelity to the proof, comes up and announces to Cloris that her brother is dead. Mélite, hearing this and being reproached by Lisis with having broken her lover's heart and caused his death by her faithlessness, falls in a swoon.

6

Her neighbor, Cliton, whom Éraste had employed to deliver the fictitious letters, coming upon the scene at this juncture, is stricken with remorse as he hears and sees the serious results of the stratagem, and mistaking this fainting spell for death, hastens to tell Éraste that his "accursed deception" has killed both Tircis and Mélite.

At this dreadful news Éraste goes mad. He imagines that he is sinking down to Tartarus and that he must seek the shades of the two lovers murdered by his artifice and pour out his blood at their feet. Thinking now that he has arrived at the banks of the Styx, he addresses Cliton for Charon, and demands passage in his boat. In vain does Cliton strive to call back to reason the demented lover. Éraste crying out :

"What! thou wishest to escape to the other side without me ?
Then I must pass over, in spite of thee, on thy neck"—

springs upon the astonished man's shoulders, and rains down upon his head a storm of blows.

Soon afterwards Éraste, from whom Cliton has escaped, meets Philandre. Mistaking him for Minos, the madman makes a clean breast of his guilty ruse.

Thus, by a skillful device whose ingenuity does much to atone for this silly pagan madness of Éraste, and which Corneille, even after he had written his great masterpieces, still regarded with pardonable pride, Philandre is undeceived and a dénoûment provided.

After Philandre leaves him, Éraste declares war against all hell. He even threatens, if Pluto opposes him in his designs, to carry off Proserpine from between the very arms of her lord.

In the next scene, which is the last of the fourth act, Lisis, explaining the purpose of his little deceit, tells Cloris that her brother is quite safe.

Here the principal action of the piece really ends, for the way is evidently cleared for a complete understanding between Tircis and Mélite.

The only remaining question—that as to the authorship of the spurious letters—may be supposed to be solved by Philandre who, to clear his own skirts as far as possible, would very naturally tell Cloris what he had found out from the ravings of Éraste, while she, just as naturally, would tell the others interested.

So, as Corneille admits, "All the fifth act may pass as useless." In that act, indeed, Éraste, cured of his madness by the announcement made to him by Mélite's nurse that the two lovers whom he believes dead are still living, becomes fully reconciled to them, and offers his heart and hand, evidently not in vain, to the fair Cloris who has just spurned from her the luckless Philandre in spite of his earnest entreaties and professed repentance. But all this constitutes only, to quote Corneille's words, "une action épisodique," and is, therefore, superfluous now that the main action has closed.

Several other defects have already been noticed in the course of our brief synopsis of the play. Only one more needs be mentioned here. That pertains to Éraste's conception of his plot to make a breach between Mélite and Tircis. How could Éraste know, first, that Philandre would credit the letters, second, that he would show them to Tircis, and third, that Tircis would without investigation also allow himself to be deceived? Yet, if all three of these conditions had not been fulfilled, Éraste's trick would have been futile. To choose thus as the mainspring of the action an intrigue against whose execution lay the strongest antecedent probability, was an error which Corneille himself has plainly pointed out.

Mélite, though very successful, did not escape adverse criticism. The craft condemned it as violating the unity of time, as wanting in incident, and as written in a vein too simple and familiar.

Corneille's answer to those who thus found fault with his *coup d'essai* was the production, in 1632, of his tragedy Clitandre, a veritable monstrosity, but rigorously restricted to twenty-four hours in its action, surcharged with startling effects, and more stilted in style. Thirty years later, in his " *examen de Clitandre,*" the poet declared that, animated "by a sort of bravado," he had in writing this drama deliberately striven to compose a play which, though quite regular, should be utterly worthless.

It is entirely possible that by that time the great genius who had produced *Le Cid* and *Rodogune,* being unable to put himself back into the mental posture which was his in 1632, had, indeed, in the course of so many years come to look upon " Clitandre," not at all as a serious effort of a young man anxious to please his public and prove his ability to conform to all their canons of criticism, however erroneous

6*

he might feel them to be, but as merely a good-humored thrust at his Bœotian critics and a self-sacrificing attempt to teach them a lesson in taste.

While, however, such may have been Corneille's honest opinion in 1662 as to the origin and purpose of *Clitandre*, we can not but believe that when he wrote the play in 1632 his chief object, and naturally, too, was to increase his popularity, though he very probably designed, also, incidentally to instruct the public by making it clearly apparent to them through a liberal exhibition of talent that the defects which his tragedy contained could not be charged to any lack of power on his part, but that they were the necessary results of the vicious style which he had for the nonce condescended to employ in order that he might demonstrate the fact that even when thus clogged and clamping he could still outstrip his contemporaries.

But whatever view may be adopted as to the point which we have just been considering, there can be no difference of opinion with regard to the merits or rather demerits of "Clitandre." It is, taken altogether, simply execrable. Among the sensational incidents in which the piece abounds is an attempt at rape occurring on the stage and foiled by the courage of the girl who thrusts her hairpin into the eye of her villainous assailant. Thus did Corneille reach the nadir of his degradation.

Fortunately his abasement was but temporary. *Clitandre* was his only effort in this lamentable style of drama. Thenceforth he refused ever again to wear the yoke of a vitiated public taste, and resolutely persisted in obeying the dictates of his own increasing experience and ripening judgment.

His next four pieces *La Veuve* (1633), *La Galerie du Palais* (1634), *La Suivante* (1634), and *La Place Royale* (1635) were comedies.

While they were all poor plays belonging to the same species as *Mélite*, they were marked by some considerable improvements which gave proof of the dramatist's growing power. More skill was shown in the construction of his plot, the characters were better differentiated, the style was a little more natural, and everything like indecency was rigorously excluded.

But there was naught as yet to tell the playwrights contemporary with Corneille how great a rival had stepped upon the stage to dispute with them the prize of fame.

His first six plays were, however, far from being profitless to him.   Beside affording him needed mental gymnastics by way of training for his great career, these early dramas, which now seem to us such feeble productions, brought him money enough to form the nucleus of his fortune and earned for him no little renown as a poet.

Richelieu, perceiving that the young author was full of promise, chose him to be one of the band of five dramatists, whose duty it was to work under the Cardinal's direction, realize his ideas and complete plays sketched by him in outline.   The other four members of this band were Boisrobert, Colletet, l'Étoile and Rotrou.

Though thus admitted to the presence and favor of the greatest statesman in Europe, Corneille found the service of the Cardinal in some respects not over pleasant.   Richelieu proved rather a hard master.

"Sa manie de faire faire des pièces, dont il faisait le plan et rimait quelques scènes, était," says Michelet, " despotique, irritante ; ces pauvres rimeurs à grand' peine tiraient la charrue sous l'aiguillon de ce terrible camarade."

His Eminence carried into the republic of letters the imperious spirit of the autocratic minister. He liked not to be crossed or corrected. Originality and independence on the part of his little coterie of poets were, in fact, tabooed. Corneille, as we shall see, could not long bear the badge of this subjection. His self-respect soon compelled him to resign his position as one of the *cinq auteurs*.

Before quitting the Cardinal's employ, however, the poet produced, in 1635, his second tragedy, *Médée*. In this piece for the first time we meet some touches of that sublimity which is the peculiar excellence of the great Corneille.

Probably our author had been roused to a consciousness of his own glorious endowment of talent, and his conception of the nature of tragedy had been not a little exalted by reflection upon the decided merits of Jean Mairet's *Sophonisbe*, a tragedy which, as we said in a former chapter, appeared about 1633, and which, lying amid that writer's weary waste of worse than mediocre dramas, reminds one strongly of a blooming, fountful oasis in a dreary desert.

Sophonisbe was planned according to the precepts of the ancients, and contained some undeniable examples of power, beauty and pathos. How so notable a piece should have come from so ordinary an author must remain something of a mystery. It would almost seem that fortune herself, smitten with an Ariadne's love for him, had thus put into his hands the thread to lead him out of the labyrinth of bad taste. But Mairet was altogether incapable of following the clue.

The excellencies of *Sophonisbe*, however, when like good seed they fell into Corneille's fertile brain, failed not to bring forth fruit an hundred fold. All at once, as by a revelation, the great poet perceived the grand possibilities of the drama. It was under the spur of this elevated ideal that he made a study of Seneca and composed *Médée*, an imitation of the Roman writer's *Medea*.

The reader is familiar with the classic legend upon which the play is based. Jason, whose father Aeson, king of Iolcus in Thessaly, had been dethroned by his half-brother Pelias, lays claim on attaining his maturity to his father's kingdom. Pelias agrees to yield up the sovereignty to Jason, provided the latter shall first bring from Aea or Colchis, the golden fleece which was suspended from a tree in the grove of Ares and guarded by an ever-vigilant dragon.

Accepting this condition and taking with him about fifty of the most famous heroes of Greece, Jason embarked in the ship Argo, and sailed for Aea.

Here after many adventures the Argonautae arrive. When they make known their mission, Aeëtes, king of the country, consents to let them have the golden fleece, if Jason will, alone, plough a piece of land with two fire-breathing, brazen-footed oxen, sow in the furrows the remainder of the teeth of the dragon which Cadmus had killed, and then slay the armed warriors who will spring up from these teeth.

This exploit of dire difficulty Jason is enabled to perform through the help of the king's daughter, Medea, a sorceress, who is deeply enamored of the young hero.

In the mean time Aeëtes is scheming to burn the Argo and slay her crew. His efforts, however, are vain. Medea, by her magical powers, puts to sleep the dragon which guards the golden fleece, Jason obtains the object of his search, and he and his comrades set sail at night, taking with them Medea and her young brother Absyrtus. Aeëtes follows them in swift pursuit. When he begins to draw near to the fugitives, Medea slays her brother, cuts his corpse into pieces and throws them into the sea, causing her father to stop in his course that he may rescue from the waves the scattered limbs of his boy.

At last, when they have experienced various adventures, Jason and Medea reach Iolcus in safety. Jason does not, however, receive his throne.

Here Medea again displays her skill in sorcery. First, she rejuvenates the aged Aeson, who, according to one account, was still living. Then she courts the confidence of the daughters of Pelias, and changing a ram into a lamb in their presence by boiling the animal in a caldron, she succeeds in persuading them to cut their father up and boil him also, promising that he shall thus be made young again. Of course the sorceress did not restore her husband's foe to life.

In punishment for this crime both Jason and

Medea were banished from Iolcus by Acastus, son of Pelias. The exiles sought refuge in Corinth. Here they spent several happy years together. But at length Jason determined to abandon Medea that he might wed Creusa or Glauce, daughter of Creon, king of Corinth.

Then was Medea wrought up into a frenzy of rage. She destroys her hated rival Creusa by sending her a poisoned robe which on being put on burns her to death, and consumes in its fatal flames her father also. Nor is Medea's mad craving for vengeance yet satisfied. Heedless of the pleadings of her mother's heart, she murders her two boys with a dagger, in order thus to fill to overflowing their father's bitter cup of grief.

Her inhuman fury satiated, Medea now escapes to Athens in a chariot drawn by winged dragons. Such is the theme of *Médée*. The scene of the play is at Corinth whither Jason and Médée have fled to escape the ire of Acastus.

I select a few striking passages which exhibit well the growing power of the poet. After Jason has disclosed his perfidious design of deserting his wife, Médée, in the fourth scene of the first act,

7

makes the following passionate appeal to the " dii conjugales : "

"Sovereign protectors of the laws of marriage,
  Ye gods, warranters of the faith that Jason has pledged me,
  Ye whom he called to witness with an immortal ardor,
  When by a false oath he conquered my modesty,
  Behold with what scorn his perjury treats you,
  And aid me to avenge this common injury ;
  If he can to-day drive me forth with impunity,
  You are without power or without resentment."

" Voici des vers," cries Voltaire, " qui annoncent Corneille ! "

The fact that our author is here following in the footsteps of Seneca can not cancel the Frenchman's claim to honor. Seneca is his teacher in tragedy, not his tyrant; Corneille is no servile copyist; he imitates, it is true, but not unfrequently he embellishes the original thought with some sublime conception of his own expressed in noble verse. Thus in the passage just quoted the forceful line

" Et m'aidez à venger cette COMMUNE injure,"

belongs not to Seneca ; it is Corneille's own in fee simple.

A little further on Médée exclaims:

> "Can he really leave me after so many services?
> Dares he really leave me after so many crimes?"

These lines, too, so plain and yet so profound and so full of power, are the product of our poet's genius and his alone.

The next remarkable passage, the most famous in the play, occurs in the fifth scene, between Médée and the attendant Nérine:

Nérine.

Compel the blindness by which you are misled,
To see to what condition fate has reduced you.
Your country hates you, your husband is faithless;
In such a great reverse what remains to you?

Médée.

Myself!
Myself, I say, and that is enough.

Nérine.

What? You alone, madam?

Médée.

Yes, thou beholdest in me alone sword and flame,
Land and sea, hell and heaven,
The sceptre of kings and the thunderbolt of the gods.

What conciseness, what vigor, what sublimity! Compare Corneille's "myself"—moi—with Seneca's "Medea superest." Who can fail to see how far the Frenchman has excelled his Roman rival here?

This *moi*, which rang through France like a bugle blast proclaiming the arrival of the tragic muse, woke responsive echoes in many a heart. The reason for the popularity of the passage is not far to seek.

France, sternly held in hand by Richelieu, still cherished in the midst of her political subjection and religious apathy an exalted ideal of dauntless heroism, chivalrous individuality, firm self-reliance. Médée's sublime "Moi" is the very concretion of this knightly sentiment. No wonder, then, that all France applauded.

It is interesting to note in this connection that the point of departure of Descartes's philosophy, as well as of Corneille's poetry, was an appeal to personality.

"Je pense, donc je suis"—it is the philosopher crying "Moi, moi, dis–je, et c'est assez." Corneille and Descartes, twin brothers they—the one in poetry, the other in prose—stand on history's chiseled pedestal, as the two formative factors in French letters during the first half of the seventeenth century.

Michelet finds in the bold " Moi " of Médée an unintentional affront to Cardinal Richelieu. " Ce moi," exclaims the brilliant historian, " n'était que le duel. Précisément la chose que le ministre poursuivait, punissait de mort."

Did the proud prelate feel the shock of this subtle antagonism ? Did he imagine that he discovered in the lines of the dramatist a spirit of revolt ? Is this a filament of the root of bitterness which was soon to spring up between the statesman and the poet? Perhaps; we may not speak with more assurance.

This play contains another section well worthy of study ; I mean the second scene of the second act. Médée there argues with king Creon against a decree which he has issued banishing her from his realm. The passage is notable throughout for strength of thought, energy of expression and skill in dialectic fencing. Many of the lines which fall from the lips of the disputants are stamped with the die of a powerful mind.

Evidently this piece, from which we have not space to quote more, is the prelude to far sublimer strains. Corneille's genius is about to be made manifest in all its glorious effulgence.

7*

Médée is, indeed, marred by grievous faults. In a measure, as Voltaire remarks, Corneille "était encore subjugué par son siècle." Glaring errors of taste are still found in his work. The childish request of Creusa for Médée's robe is unworthy of the stern style of tragedy. Old Aegée, king of Athens, who offers his heart to Creusa, only to be contemned by her, and who afterward, for an attempt to carry her off by force, is shut up by her partisans in a prison whence he is delivered by the art of Médée, is a character at once uninteresting and ridiculous.

Some of the declamatory passages are tiresome from their length, a fault equally chargeable upon Seneca's Medea. But in spite of all such blemishes, *Médée* is still, intrinsically, a vigorous, though unequal tragedy, adorned here and there with bright jewels of thought, while historically the play is a waymark on the road of progress indicating a notable advance in the direction of good taste.

CHAPTER III.

THE FULL BLOOM OF GENIUS: LE CID.

WE have now reached the never-to-be-forgotten year 1636. Fame with busy fingers is weaving a fadeless chaplet for our poet. Corneille is writing " Le Cid." He has lost the favor of his great protector, the Cardinal. It happened in this wise. Richelieu, about the close of 1635, put into the hands of his five poets a comedy called *Les Tuileries,* whose scenes he had himself arranged. Corneille, to whom the third act had been given, had the hardihood to make some needed change in that part of the piece. The prime minister was much displeased. Two jealous and unworthy colleagues of the offending poet eagerly added fuel to the flame of Richelieu's resentment. He told Corneille sharply that he must have " un esprit de suite "—must be more complaisant and submissive, a sort of literary serf. Whereupon Corneille with dignity retired from membership as

75

one of the *cinq auteurs*, and withdrew to Rouen.
Here following the advice of M. de Châlon, some-
time secretary to the queen-mother Marie de Medici,
he devoted himself to the study of the Spanish language and literature.

The marriage of Louis XIII in 1615 to Anne of
Austria, daughter of Philip III of Spain, had made
the influence of the latter country a potent factor in
the fashions, society and letters of the time. Spanish
was as necessary a part of polite education in France
as French is to-day in England.

The dramatists, as we saw in a former chapter,
had not hesitated to draw upon the fund of foreign
genius thus placed at their disposal in the literature
of Castile. Drama after drama had been imitated
from the stage of Madrid. The playwrights strove
to transport into France the brilliant stage effects,
the stirring romance, the oriental pomp, the extravagant hyperbole, the high-flown metaphors which
characterized the Spanish style. Thus far, however,
the French freebooters had shown but little taste
or judgment in the use of their captured treasure.
They did not go to Spain for inspiration simply.
They went thither for matter and manner both.

What was the result? They caught the tone of Spanish exaggeration, but they could not appropriate that glowing imagination which colors Spanish literature with gorgeous hues, even as the warm sun colors a garden of the tropics.

In the hands of Frenchmen Castilian pomp degenerates into pomposity and bold figures into vapid fustian. What more could be expected?

Between France and Spain, both in character and environment, there was a great difference. In the passionate nation who lived beneath the splendor of a southern sky—a nation through whose veins coursed the mingled blood of the brave and dignified Celtiberian, the fierce but withal chivalrous Goth and the fervent, fanciful Arab—a nation whose past was rich in heroic deeds and whose prestige was still great among the peoples of Europe—in such a nation a courtly manner, sometimes lapsing into the grandiose, a flowery diction, a picturesque extravagance, were natural and therefore pardonable.

But this style was not suited to France. Behind her were different traditions; within her dwelt a different spirit; the elements of her national life were different. What wonder then that her authors, while they imitated all too successfully the artifice, affectation and obscurity of Gongora and his school, either missed or marred the real beauties of the Spanish theatre.

Corneille, however, is now studying that theatre to far better purpose. His mind is soon impressed by the great dramatic possibilities presented by a play of Guillen de Castro, the subject of which is the national hero of Spain, Rodrigo Diaz, called by his grateful countrymen El Cid Campeador, or the Lord Champion.

Corneille, finding in the popularity of the Spanish drama a voucher which he sought for his own success, at once determines to compose a piece upon the same theme.

Before passing to the delightful task of reviewing that piece, we must pause for an instant to chronicle the appearance in 1636 of " L'Illusion Comique," a very poor play, containing, it is true, some fine lines, but as a whole misshapen, disfigured by far-fetched conceits, and entirely unworthy of Corneille.

He himself calls it " un étrange monstre," and Voltaire declares " Cette pièce mérite véritablement le nom que lui donne Corneille, et pouvait être

regardée comme un sommeil de l'auteur après la
tragédie de Médée: mais," continues the commen-
tator, "quel réveil que la pièce du Cid, qui suivit
immédiatement cette farce!" It was indeed a great
awakening—an awakening to undying fame. Never
in the history of French literature has there been
such an epoch-making or such an epoch-marking
play as the *Cid*. From the god-like brain of Corneille it sprang forth in all its peerless beauty, like
Pallas from the majestic brow of the cloud-compel-
ling Zeus. The poet had made no mistake in the
choice of his subject. The ermined honor of the
Cid as, to punish the insult inflicted upon his aged
father, he yields up all hope of wedding her who
was to him the half of his soul; the devoted duty of
Chimène, who in her turn like an inexorable yet
adorable Fury seeks vengeance on her lover for
the slaughter of her father; the leal love which still
lives in all its tender power in both these lancinated
hearts—such were the passionate principles to be
portrayed in conflict dire. The whole story was
informed with the very spirit of drama. How well
Corneille has mixed his colors, how vividly his
master's brush has brought out all the beauty and

the pathos, all the nobility and the power, all the
lights and the shades of the battle, is plain to the
most untutored eye.

But without further preface let us turn to the
play.   From Elvire, her governess, Chimène learns
with tremulous joy that she has the permission of
her father, Don Gomès, Count of Gormas, to follow
the dictates of her own heart in the choice of a husband.   Both of the cavaliers suing for her hand are
worthy of her, so the count says in his interview
with Elvire.   Of Don Rodrigue, especially, upon
whom Chimène has bestowed all the boundless
wealth of her best affections, he speaks in the highest terms, declaring that the young knight

> "Goes forth from a house so prolific in warriors
> That they are there born in the midst of laurels,"

and paying a high tribute to the worth of Rodrigue's
father, Don Diègue.   How happy is Chimène at
hearing these glad tidings.   But, like the swift
shadow that flits across the flowery meads in. May,
a vague foreboding for a moment overcasts her
ecstasy of bliss.   This presentiment, alas! is to be
realized only too soon.

The king appoints as tutor of his son Don Diègue, ignoring the claims of Don Gomès who greatly desired the office. The latter nobleman is so piqued at his disappointment that he rejects with insults the request which, in behalf of Rodrigue, Don Diègue makes for the hand of Chimène. In the dialogue between the two fathers who boast not without a certain grave dignity, the one of past achievements, the other of present prowess, Corneille admirably depicts that haughty pride which was such a prominent feature in the character of Castilian cavaliers. The dispute waxes warmer.

At length, overcome with chagrin and irritation, Don Gomès strikes Don Diègue upon the cheek. The poor old man is powerless to repay the blow. Don Gomès snatches from his trembling hand his useless sword, but at once returns it, and then withdraws with a last cruel taunt. The utter humiliation of Don Diègue is pitiable to look upon.

> "Oh rage! oh despair!" he cries, "oh hateful old age!
> Have I then lived so long only for this infamy?
> And have I grown gray in the toils of war
> Only to see so many laurels wither in one day?"

8

Then he remembers that there is one who will maintain for him the honor of his storied name and wipe out in blood the stain upon his hitherto spotless glory—that one is his son Rodrigue. When, therefore, the young man, his soul all filled with "the purple light of love," comes with joyous step and eager expectation to greet his father and receive from him the formal consent of Don Gomès to the marriage of the lovers, Don Diègue startles the would-be bridegroom with the unexpected question:

"Rodrigue, hast thou any courage?"

With the impetuous spirit of youth the son replies:

"Any other than my father should test it at once."

Don Diègue, rejoiced at this flash of fire which argues a heart true as steel, then exclaims:

"Come my son, come my blood; come to repair my shame;
Come to avenge me."

"Of what?" cries the astonished Rodrigue.
"Of an affront so cruel," answers the galled father,

"That upon the honor of us both it inflicts a mortal wound;
Of a blow."

He warns Rodrigue that his foe is no mean antagonist :

"I have seen him, all covered with blood and dust,
  Carry terror everywhere into an entire army;
  I have seen by his valor a hundred squadrons broken;
  And still to tell you something more,
  More than a brave soldier, more than a great captain,
  He is —"

"I pray you finish," Rodrigue bursts forth as a suspicion of the awful truth dawns upon him.   Then Don Diègue completes his sentence with the dread words :

"The father of Chimène."

Don Rodrigue.

The —

Don Diègue.

Reply not, I know thy love;
But he who can live dishonored is unworthy of life;
The dearer the offender, the greater the offense.
In short thou knowest the offense and thou dost hold the vengeance.
I tell thee nothing more.   Avenge me, avenge thyself;
Show thyself a son worthy of a father such as I.

Rodrigue, whose soul is torn with agony, thus bemoans his unhappy position in a lyric monologue which pulsates, palpitates with passion :

"Pierced even to the bottom of the heart
By a blow unforeseen as well as mortal,
Miserable avenger of a just quarrel,
And unfortunate object of an unjust rigor,
I remain motionless and my dejected soul
Yields to the blow which slays me.
So near to seeing my love rewarded,
Oh! God, the strange pain!
In this affront my father is the offended
And the offender the father of Chimène.

"What hard struggles I feel!
Against my own honor my love is interested;
It is necessary to avenge a father and lose a lover;
The one animates my heart, the other restrains my arm.
Reduced to the sad choice either to betray my love,
Or to live dishonored,
In either case my misfortune is infinite:
O God! the strange pain!
Must I leave an affront unpunished?
Must I punish the father of Chimène?

"Father, lover; honor, love;
Noble and hard constraint, amiable tyranny;
All my pleasures are dead, or my glory tarnished;

The one renders me unhappy, the other unworthy of life.
Dear and cruel hope of a soul noble,
But at the same time amorous;
Worthy enemy of my greatest good fortune,
Sword which causest my pain;
Art thou given me to avenge mine honor?
Art thou given me to lose me my Chimène?

"Then it is better to rush to death.
I owe a duty to my love as well as to my father:
In avenging myself I attract her hate and her wrath;
Her scorn I attract in not avenging myself.
One course renders me faithless to my sweetest hope,
And the other unworthy of her.
My misfortune increases by wishing to cure it;
All redoubles my pain.
Come, my soul, and since it is necessary to die,
Let us die at least without offending Chimène.

"To die without obtaining my satisfaction!
To seek a death so fatal to my glory!
To endure that Spain shall charge my memory
With having ill sustained the honor of my house!
To respect a love of which my distempered soul
Sees the destruction assured!
Let us listen no longer to this corrupting thought
Which only serves to increase my pain.
Come, my arm, let us save honor at least,
Since after all I must lose Chimène.

8*

> "Yes, my mind was deceived:
> I owe all to my father before my mistress.
> Whether I die in combat or die of sorrow,
> I will give back my blood as pure as I have received it.
> I accuse myself already of too much negligence:
>   Let us run to vengeance;
> And, all ashamed for having hesitated so much,
> Let us no longer be in pain,
> Since to-day my father is the offended,
> Though the offender *is* the father of Chimène."

This splendid passage shows how Corneille could smite the quivering chords in the human heart, that harp of many strings.

In accordance with his stern determination Rodrigue meets and slays the father of his beloved. Then there arises a terrible strife in the bosom of Chimène. All the emotions of her soul are polarized around duty and love. She must bring to justice the slayer of her father. But Rodrigue is the criminal! How can she shed the blood whose every drop is dearer to her than oriental ruby? Yet she does decide to follow duty, and hastens to the king to demand that Rodrigue be compelled to pay the extreme penalty of his crime.

"Sire," she cries, "Sire, justice!
He has slain my father."
"He has avenged his own," pleads Don Diègue.

And thus the maiden begs as a boon her lover's
death ; thus the gray-haired father implores pardon
for his dauntless son ; while all the spectators in
suspense know not what the end will be. The
king, however, delays his decision, promising that
justice shall eventually be done.

How wretched now is Rodrigue! Like lurid
lightning his terrible trouble has scorched and
seared his soul; the apples that grow in Love's
garden are ashen to his taste, the cypress waves
where roses bloomed, and from the spray on which
sat and sang the nightingale now croaks the bird
of doom. With crushed heart he goes to the
home of Chimène, himself to offer her the life
which she demands. To Elvire who expresses
her amazement at seeing him there, the sorrow-
stricken youth replies:

"Regard me no more with astonished face;
I seek death after having inflicted it.
My judge is my love, my judge is my Chimène;
I merit death for meriting her hate;

And I come to receive as a sovereign boon
Both the death-sentence from her mouth and the death-blow
     from her hand.''

Rodrigue withdraws for a time, and Chimène entering thus describes the anguished contest in her bosom to Elvire :

" It is too little to say love, Elvire, I adore him ;
   My passion opposes my resentment ;
   In my enemy I find my lover ;
   And I feel that in spite of all my wrath
   Rodrigue in my heart still combats my father :
   He attacks him, he presses him, he yields, he defends himself,
   Now strong, now feeble and now triumphant :
   But in this hard combat of anger and love,
   He harrows my heart without dividing my purpose ;
   And whatever power my love may have over me,
   I hesitate not to follow my duty ;
   I hasten without deliberation where honor constrains me.
   Rodrigue is very dear to me, his fate afflicts me ;
   My heart takes his part ; but against its influence
   I know that I am a daughter and that my father is dead."

In vain does Elvire attempt to dissuade her from her tragic determination, exclaiming at length,

     " But you love Rodrigue, he can not displease you."

Chimène.

I confess it.

Elvire.

After all, what think you then to do ?

Chimène.

In order to preserve my glory and end my grief,
To pursue him, to destroy him, and after him to die.

Now ensues one of the most dramatic scenes in
literature. Rodrigue, the crowned king of her
heart, Rodrigue, the abhorred slayer of her father,
presents himself to Chimène, bearing in his hand
the sword still crimson with that father's blood.
Hear the dialogue between these two who have so
fondly loved, who have so pitifully lost :

Rodrigue.

Ah well, without troubling yourself to pursue,
Assure yourself the honor of taking my life.

Chimène.

Elvire, where are we ? and what do I see ?
Rodrigue in my house ! Rodrigue before me !

Rodrigue.

Spare not my blood; taste without resistance
The sweetness of my destruction and of your vengeance.

Chimène.

Alas!

Rodrigue.

Listen to me.

Chimène.

I die.

Rodrigue.

A moment.

Chimène.

Go, let me die.

Rodrigue.

Four words only;
Afterwards answer me only with this sword.

Chimène.

What! all reeking still with my father's blood!

Rodrigue.

My Chimène . . . .

Chimène.

Take from me this odious object
Which brings before my eyes the reproach of thy crime and
thy life.

Rodrigue.

Look at it rather to excite thy hate,
To increase thy wrath and to hasten my punishment.

Chimène.

It is stained with my blood.

Rodrigue.

Plunge it into mine;
And make it lose thus the tint of thine.

Chimène.

Ah! what cruelty which kills in one day
The father by the sword, the daughter by the sight!
Take from me this object, I can not endure it:
You wish me to hear you and you make me die.

Rodrigue then declares that he does not repent of
his action. He has only walked in the plain path
of honor. Yet his love is not less strong. It had
made him, a knight of Castile, hesitate as to whether
he should avenge a mortal affront. Doubtless, he

says, his powerful passion would have made him forget his glory had he not known that Chimène would have scorned a lover who bore the brand of shame. In concluding his explanation Rodrigue says :

> " I have done what I ought, and what I ought I do ;
>   I know that a dead father arms thee against my crime ;
>   I have not wished to deprive thee of thy victim.
>   Immolate with courage to the blood that thy father has lost
>   Him who glories in having shed it."

Chimène replies that she does not blame him, she only weeps for her misfortune. But his laudable course has marked out clearly her duty, too. He avenged a father's injured honor, she must avenge a father's blood.

> " Alas ! " she cries in an outburst of pathetic grief, " thy fate
>   here puts me in despair.
> If some other misfortune had snatched from me my father,
> My soul would have found in the boon of seeing thee
> The one solace that it would have been able to receive ;
> And against my sorrow I would have felt some charms
> When a hand so dear dried my tears.
> But I must lose thee after having lost him ;
> This effort against my love to my honor is due ;

And this dreadful duty, whose command assassinates me,
Compels me myself to work for thy ruin."

Rodrigue now urges Chimène to cut short his miserable days, but she refuses, saying,

" I am thy adversary, and not thy executioner."
" My hand alone," Rodrigue argues, " has known how to avenge
the insult to my father,
Thy hand alone ought to avenge thine."
"Cruel !" cries Chimène, " why be obstinate upon that point ?
Thou hast avenged thyself without aid and thou wishest to
aid me !
I will follow thy example and I have too much courage
To suffer that my glory be divided with thee.
My father and my honor will not consent to owe anything
To the promptings either of thy love or of thy despair."

" In the name of a dead father," Rodrigue pleads, " or of our
friendship
Punish me in vengeance or at least in pity.
Thy unhappy lover will have much less pain
To die by thy hand than to live with thy hate."

Chimène.

Go, I hate thee not.

Rodrigue.

Thou oughtest.

9

Chimène.

I can not.

Again Rodrigue urges her to kill him, and again she refuses.

Rodrigue.

On what art thou resolved ?

Chimène.

In spite of the love so beautiful which disturbs my wrath,
I will do my best to avenge well my father;
But despite the rigor of so cruel a duty
My one desire is to be able to do nothing.

Rodrigue.

O ! miracle of love !

Chimène.

O ! acme of woe !

Rodrigue.

How many ills and tears our fathers cost us !

Chimène.

Rodrigue, who would have believed it . . . . .

Rodrigue.

Chimène, who would have said it . . . . .

Chimène.

That our happiness should be so near and should be lost so soon.

Rodrigue.

And that so near to haven, against all appearance,
A storm so sudden should break our hope?

Chimène.

Oh, mortal griefs!

Rodrigue.

Oh, useless regrets!

Chimène.

Go away, once again, I hear thee no more.

Rodrigue.

Farewell! I go to drag out a dying life
Until by thy pursuit it be taken from me.

Chimène.

If I succeed in it, I engage thee my faith
To breathe not a moment after thee.
Farewell; depart, and above all take good care not to be seen.

[*Rodrigue goes out.*]

Elvire.

Madam, whatever ills heaven may send upon us . . . . .

Chimène.

Importune me no more, let me sigh ;
I seek silence and night to weep.

After this heart-rending interview Rodrigue meets
his father who gives him a guerdon of grateful
praise, and urges him at the same time to stifle
his love for Chimène. But this Rodrigue will
not, this he can not do. Her name is chiseled on
his heart in imperishable letters. To her, moreover, he is bound by a sentiment of honor not less
lofty and exacting than that which drove him to
slay her father. The noble young knight can not
break his plighted word, neither can he hope to wed
the woman of his love. Death, therefore, seems the
only portal of exit from his sorrow.

But his father, telling him that a Moorish fleet
menaces the city with immediate attack and striving
with the gleaming torch of glory to dissipate the
darkness of despair which has settled down upon
the soul of his son, bids him obey his country's
clarion call, and thus win the favor of the king and,
perhaps, the forgiveness of Chimène, or at least a
hero's glorious death and a patriot's deathless fame.

Rodrigue heeds the appeal. The warrior's spirit within him wakes. With five hundred heroes who had assembled to avenge the affront offered to Don Diègue, and whose ranks were soon swelled to three thousand, the gallant youth, stilling for a moment with imperious command the wild waves of lovelorn woe that surge over his soul, rushes forth,

"tiger-passioned, lion-thoughted,"

Go p.v.

to pour out, if need be, his heart's blood as a libation upon his country's hallowed altar.

In the gloom of the night this Spartan band meets the Moorish host. Then and there amid the clang of armor, the clash of swords and the clamor of embattled soldiery, Rodrigue, by prodigies of bravery rescues his country from peril, and wins an exalted place in poetry's pantheon of deified patriots. The report of this famous victory runs like wild-fire through all the city. Chimène, learning from the faithful Elvire of the glorious news, exclaims in tender pride:

" And the hand of Rodrigue has wrought all these miracles ! "

Then, as she thinks of the manifold dangers of

9*

the battle, with changing color and fearful voice, she hastens to ask,

> "But is he not wounded?"

Elvire assures her that there is no news of such mishap. Thereupon duty again grapples love with iron grasp, and, like Grecian athletes in an Olympic contest, these powerful emotions struggle for master-dom. Duty conquers. The cooing voice of love is drowned in the bosom of Chimène by the serpent hisses of revenge.

> "If he *has* vanquished two kings," she cries in a wild transport
> of rage,
> "If he has vanquished two kings, he has slain my father."

Duty conquers, but oh! at what cost of suffering to Chimène! The higher Rodrigue rises on the sun-gilded, far-gleaming peaks of fame, the more dismal seems the dread abysm of despair in which she languishes. His worth increased does but increase her loss.

Now Rodrigue, having received permission to recount the story of his great exploit to the king, describes with nervous eloquence and in graphic style the glorious battle. Beginning with the request that the king will pardon him for acting without the royal authority, and urging in excuse the imminence of the peril and the fact that he could not come to the court without risking his life—a life which he would far rather yield fighting for his sovereign—the young soldier thus continues :

" Under me, then, this troop advances,
And they bear upon their brows a bold assurance.
We set out five hundred strong; but, by a prompt reinforcement,
We saw ourselves three thousand on arriving at the port;
So much courage did the most terrified regain
At seeing us march with such a mien!
I conceal two-thirds of them as soon as they arrive,
In the holds of the vessels which were then found there:
The rest, whose number increased every hour,
Burning with impatience, remain around me,
Lie down on the earth, and, without making any noise,
Pass a good part of the beautiful night.
By my command the guard does the same,
And, keeping themselves concealed, aid my stratagem ;
And I boldly pretend to have received from you
The order which they see me follow and which I give to all.
That obscure light which falls from the stars
At last with the flood tide lets us see thirty sail;
The wave swells beneath them, and, with a common impulse,
The Moors and the sea move onward to the port.

We let them pass; all appears tranquil to them;
No soldiers at the port, none on the walls of the city.
Our profound silence deceiving their minds,
They dare no longer doubt of having surprised us;
They approach without fear, they anchor, they disembark,
And run to deliver themselves into the hands that await them.
We rise then, and all at the same time
Raise to heaven a thousand piercing shouts,
Our men from our ships respond to these cries;
They appear armed, the Moors are confounded;
Terror seizes them when half disembarked;
Before fighting they believe themselves lost.
They were running to pillage and they encountered war;
We press them on the water, we press them on land,
And we make rivulets of their blood run,
Before one of them can resist or regain his rank.
But very soon, in spite of us, their princes rally them;
Their courage revives and their terrors are forgotten.
The shame of dying without having fought
Stops their disorder, and gives them back their valor.
Against us with firm foot they draw their simitars;
They make horrible mixtures of our blood with theirs;
And the earth and the river, and their fleet and the port
Are fields of carnage where death triumphs.
Oh, how many actions, how many fame-worthy deeds,
Have remained without glory in the midst of the darkness,
Where each one, sole witness of the great blows which he gave,
Could not see to which side fate inclined!
I went on all sides to encourage our men,

To make some advance, and to sustain the others,
To marshal those who came, urge them forward in their turn,
And I could not know the issue until the break of day.
But at last its light shows our advantage:
The Moor sees his defeat, and suddenly loses courage;
And, seeing a reinforcement coming to succor us,
The ardor of conquering yields to the fear of death,
They gain their ships, they cut their cables,
Raise to heaven frightful cries,
Retreat in tumult, and without considering
Whether their kings can retire with them.
Their terror is too strong to permit this duty;
The flood-tide brought them thither; the ebb takes them back;
While their kings, engaged among us,
And some few of their soldiers, all pierced with our strokes,
Contend valiantly and sell their lives dear.
In vain I myself invite them to surrender;
Simitar in hand, they heed me not:
But seeing all their soldiers fall at their feet,
And that, alone, henceforth they defend themselves in vain,
They ask for the chief; I announce myself; they surrender.
I send them both to you at the same time;
And the combat ceased for want of combatants.
It is in that way, that, for your service . . . . . ."

These last words of his story still flutter on his
lips, when it is announced that Chimène is coming
again to demand justice from the king. Rodrigue

retires and Chimène enters. The king, to test her feelings, pretends that Rodrigue has died of wounds received in battle, and bids Chimène thank heaven for thus avenging her. The sudden, death-like pallor that overspreads her face proves how deep is the poor girl's love.

"What!" she cries, "Rodrigue then is dead!"

"No, no," replies the king, "he lives
And for thee still preserves an unchangeable love;
Calm this grief which interests itself for him!"

But recovering her self-possession, Chimène declares that her evident emotion was due to chagrin that Rodrigue should have met his death on the field of honor instead of on the scaffold. Vainly the king pleads for Rodrigue. Chimène is implacable. Since the king will not punish her lover, she appeals to arms, calling upon all the cavaliers of the court to espouse her cause in the lists, and promising that when Rodrigue shall have fallen, she will wed his conqueror. Although, according to custom, Chimène was entitled to this trial by battle, the king at first peremptorily refuses to subject Rodrigue to the perils of successive duels with the numerous knights likely to be brought into the field by such an offer from such a maiden.

"The Moors as they fled," says the grateful monarch, "have carried away his crime."

But Don Diègue begs the king not to break the law in order to favor Rodrigue, lest such action should sully his fair fame. Reluctantly the king yields so far as to permit one combat, bidding Chimène choose well the warrior to represent her, as by the issue of this duel she must abide. She accepts Don Sanche as her champion. The contest is to take place two hours hence. In conclusion, the king, in spite of her protest, announces that upon the victor, whoever he may be, he will bestow the hand of Chimène. All now await the decisive moment. But in the meantime Rodrigue goes to take his last farewell of Chimène. It is a fine scene. Since she so resolutely seeks his death, he will not, he says, defend himself against the arm that fights for her. She tells him to remember that defeat would eclipse the splendor of his glory. Again, touching another chord, she exclaims:

"Dost thou treat my father with so much rigor
  That after having conquered him, thou dost suffer a conqueror."

But Rodrigue is deaf to all appeals, until at last, driven to extremities, she entreats him to save her from a marriage with Don Sanche; and bids him come forth "conqueror from a combat of which Chimène is the prize." At these magic words Rodrigue's heart leaps within him; every nerve quivers with joy; at last the sun bursts through the rifted clouds.

"Is there," he cries in rapture, "Is there any foe that I can not
     conquer now?
Appear Navarrese, Moors and Castilians,
And all the heroes that Spain has nourished;
Unite and make an army
To combat a hand thus incited:
Join all your efforts against a hope so sweet;
Too few are ye to succeed."

Fired by such enthusiasm 'tis but an easy task for Rodrigue to disarm his antagonist, whose life, however, he spares because it was hazarded for Chimène. Obedient to his conqueror's command, Don Sanche carries to her his sword in token of Rodrigue's victory, but she, supposing her lover fallen, receives her champion with such words as, " Perfidious one!"—"Execrable assassin!" She will hear no explanation. Her passionate love for Rodrigue finds full vent. She implores the king to release her from a loathsome union with Don Sanche. At last she learns the truth. The king urges her to pursue no more her noble lover, no more to resist the manifest will of Heaven. Rodrigue on bended knee again offers her his life. She bids him rise. She can not now deny the love she bears him. She even demurely admits that where a king commands one must obey. And yet—she shrinks back, for a father's corpse lies between them. The king, knowing the healing power of time, wisely grants her a year to balm her grief, bidding Rodrigue meantime continue his glorious career.

And thus, as the curtain falls, we feel assured that, when the uttermost farthing of duty's debt shall have been paid, the rainbow of love in brightness and beauty shall shine through the tempest of tears.

The success of the *Cid* was phenomenal. The poet received at once his accolade, not indeed by princely favor, but from a proud people. Everywhere the piece was greeted with perfect transports of enthusiasm. How just was the verdict of Corneille's countrymen, how powerfully he has depicted

10

in this piece love, honor and duty, has, I hope, been evident, even from my feeble effort. As a humble admirer of some master artist might lift a veil from the face of one of that artist's greatest paintings, so have I simply tried to lift the veil of French which hides from American eyes this magnificent picture of the *Cid*, and to let my readers see for themselves how the passions were there portrayed by Corneille.

If you ask me whether there are any faults in the *Cid*, I might reply in proverbial phrase that the sun has its spots, or quote to you the sensible words of Pope:

> "Whoever thinks a faultless piece to see,
> Thinks what ne'er was, nor is, nor e'er shall be."

Of course the *Cid* contains some defects, but you will have to read it more than once and wait until the lyric passion which its fervid eloquence and sublime poetry with their rush and roll and rhythm excite has subsided, before you can begin to perceive those blemishes. Critics generally agree in condemning as superfluous the part of the Infanta, a character whom I have not mentioned in my summary. She is represented in the first act as greatly

troubled in spirit. Secretly she loves Rodrigue.
But she can not wed him. Her royal rank forbids
that. She has, therefore, labored to bring about a
union between him and Chimène. But, alas for the
poor princess, until that marriage shall have been
finally consummated, she is doomed to be tortured by
a passion which she strives in vain to stifle. In the
second act, after speaking words of cheer to Chimène,
when the latter is dreading an encounter between
her father and Rodrigue, the Infanta lays bare her
heart to her confidant Léonor. Confessing her love
for Rodrigue, the unhappy princess tells what flattering hopes her fond heart whispers. Suppose Rodrigue should meet and conquer the Count; what
exploit after that will be too difficult for the young
hero's arm? Will he not go on from deed to deed
of valor till vanquished nations shall confess his
prowess and her love be vindicated by its object's
high renown? The Infanta does not appear in the
third act. In the fourth, she vainly entreats Chimène to sacrifice the demands of blood to the claims
of country and to desist from the prosecution of
Rodrigue, who has now become

" the pillar of a people's hope."

In the fifth act the princess, after weighing Rodrigue's fame against her pride of rank, decides that he is worthy of her, but determines to give him up to Chimène who, in spite of her cries for vengeance, is evidently devoted to him still.

> "I will conquer myself," exclaims the Infanta, "not for fear of
> any blame,
> But in order not to disturb such a beautiful love."

And so, indeed, she does. But all this is justly regarded as unnecessary and tedious, because it is something outside of the real action of the play.

Having thus pointed out the main defect in "Le Cid," we need merely say with regard to the other strictures made upon it, that they fall into two classes; first, criticisms to which an adequate defence might be opposed, and, second, criticisms which, though well-founded, are still of altogether minor importance, and which can not cloud the bright glory of this noble drama. Our limited space makes it impossible for us to notice either of these two classes further.

It is interesting to note the effect of the appearance of "Le Cid" upon French politics. In 1624,

Richelieu, seeing that the ranks of the nobility were being decimated by frequent duels, persuaded the king to issue a stringent ordinance against the custom. For disobedience to this ordinance M. de Bouteville, who was a Montmorency, and his second, the Count of Chapelles, were put to death. Richelieu, in discussing with the king the expediency of their execution, boldly exclaimed: " It is a question of breaking the neck of duels or of your Majesty's edicts ! " The Cardinal was evidently bent on eradicating the code.

Now " Le Cid " was, in some sort, a glorification of the duel ! The young Corneille, with Rodrigue's courage, appeared to be throwing down the gauntlet to "l'Éminentissime" himself! Again Richelieu since 1635 had been carrying on a war with Spain. But in " Le Cid " Spanish manners and Spanish chivalry were presented in such a blaze of glory as to call forth from every audience tumultuous applause. Well might the prime minister gnash his teeth amid the general laudation of the play. Michelet comments as follows upon the subjects to which I have just referred : " Aurait-on pu en 1637, après le Cid, ce qu'on avait pu en 1626, punir

10*

de mort l'obstiné duelliste revenu pour se battre
sous les croisées du roi? Non, l'édit était aboli, la
scène avait vaincu les lois; sur Richelieu planait
Corneille. La campagne s'ouvrait. De quel coeur
la noblesse allait-elle se battre contre les descen-
dants du Cid, ces Espagnols aimés et admirés?
Français et Espagnols allaient penser également
que l'ennemi n'était qu'à Paris, l'ennemi commun,
Richelieu."

These considerations would be sufficient to show
that "Le Cid" could never be looked upon with
approval by the Cardinal. But his sharp antipathy
to Corneille was doubtless due to a complex of
causes. Perhaps the first of these was a feeling of
resentment at Médée's bold "MOI"—that quintes-
sence of the duel, as Michelet thinks. Then came
the strain in the relations between the poet and the
prelate consequent upon the correction made by the
former in the comedy of "the Thuilleries." Corneille, a king in spirit, could but ill play the courtier.
When, therefore, the Cardinal bestowed favors upon
other dramatists, the great tragedian preserved a
dignified indifference; nay, more, in the "Excuse à
Ariste," published in 1636, before the appearance of

"Le Cid," he gloried in the fact that his increasing fame had been won by his own unaided genius.

"Mon travail," he exclaims, "sans appui monte sur le théâtre
* * * * * * * * * *
Par d'illustres avis je n'éblouis personne
* * * * * * * * * *
Je ne dois qu'à moi seul toute ma renommée."

It was probably with little patience that Richelieu heard this proud boast. But the breach, already considerable, was greatly widened by the appearance of "Le Cid." Here was a play written by a man from whom the Cardinal was estranged, exalting at once, as we have seen, the duel which he had proscribed and the Spaniards with whom he was at war, outshining far every attempt which he himself had made at dramatic composition, and setting all Paris wild with delight. Richelieu was stung to the quick. The young poet, so it seemed to the Cardinal, had dared to assume toward him, the most powerful premier in Europe, an attitude of independence, if not of absolute defiance. This rebel must be crushed, this rival must be downed.

Richelieu found willing helpers in his project. The devil of bad taste which Corneille had bidden come out of literature departed not without much wrathful writhing and rending. An atrabilious band of authors, among whom may be mentioned Scudéry, Mairet, Bois-Robert and Claveret, stood with daggers drawn ready to do to the death the reputation of the great poet. The Cardinal—alas! for his fame—debased himself so far as to encourage and set on these assassins. Scudéry, a ridiculous writer

> "dont la fertile plume
> Peut tous les mois sans peine enfanter un volume"

is chief of the cabal. He is quite beside himself with rage. He can discover little or no beauty in "Le Cid," for he sees it only through the green spectacles of jealousy. He gives vent to his venom by composing a critique upon the play, beginning his attack with this savage thrust: "There are certain pieces, like certain animals that exist in nature, which, at a distance, look like stars, and which, on close inspection, are only worms." "Le Cid" a glow-worm, forsooth! This passage is sufficient to show the spirit of Scudéry's onslaught. The same feeling of bitter envy animated the other members of the clique. The fight waxed hot and hotter.

Insults were heaped upon Corneille. Scudéry in an insolent private letter even went so far as to send him a kind of challenge. To this silly burst of spleen Corneille, who had proudly defended his fame against his enemies, made the following sensible reply: "There is no necessity for knowing how much nobler or more valiant you may be than myself, in order to judge how far superior 'Le Cid' is to the 'Amant Libéral.' . . . . I am not a fighting man; so that, in that respect, you have nothing to fear."

In all the dispute the public were true to our author.

> "En vain contre *Le Cid* un ministre se ligue,
> Tout Paris pour Chimène a les yeux de Rodrigue."

At length the Cardinal, rightly thinking that it was high time to end such a noisy and unseemly wrangle, determined to remove the case from the bar of public opinion and carry it into the court of the French Academy which he had created and from which he expected a servile decision. Accordingly he persuaded Scudéry to appeal to this tribunal for judgment upon the matter at issue. The Academy were very loath to try the case. They pointed out to the Cardinal by way of mild remonstrance the obvious risk which the infant institution would run of rendering itself hateful to the nation by assuming finally to pronounce upon the worth of so popular a piece. But it was of no avail. Richelieu declared that their reasons seemed to him of but little moment. The Academicians then advanced another objection. They reminded him that their statutes forbade them "to judge a work without the consent and request of the author." This request Corneille had not made, this consent he had not given. Determined not to be balked, Richelieu employed Bois-Robert to obtain from him the desired declaration of acquiescence in the proceeding. But Corneille with suave diplomacy maintained his position of vantage, skilfully parrying every appeal. He told Bois-Robert that the matter was quite below the dignity of the Academy, and that the establishment of such a precedent as the proposed trial of " Le Cid " was furthermore, fraught with much danger and vexation, since envious scribblers would be constantly bringing before the Academy indictments against each new piece that might win popular favor. Finally Bois-Robert found it necessary to declare in plain terms the will of Richelieu. Then Corneille saw that he must yield, and, after stating once more his objections, he added : "The gentlemen of the Academy may do as they please ; as you write that Monseigneur would be glad to have their judgment, and that it would divert his Eminence, I have nothing more to say." If Corneille seems to us to have displayed some weakness in thus surrendering, let us remember the age, the country, the civilization in which he lived. "Le moyen," cries M. Fontenelle, "Le moyen de ne pas ménager un pareil ministre, et qui était son bienfaiteur?"[1]

Richelieu greedily clutched Corneille's reluctant words as a carte blanche. But the Academy still hung back from the business. At last the tiger showed his teeth. "Tell those gentlemen that I desire it," exclaimed the Cardinal, "and that I shall love them as they love me." The Academy dare resist no longer. Theirs was a hard task, for they had on the one hand the irritated premier and on the other the enthusiastic public to conciliate. The luckless critics were thus between the Devil and the

[1] The poet was then receiving a pension from the premier.

Deep Sea, so to speak. Three times did they present to the Cardinal their report, only to have it thrice thrust back upon them as unsatisfactory. His Eminence was greatly vexed, because they could not, with any heed to their literary consciences, deal out condemnation unmixed and unmeasured upon "Le Cid." Their fourth report, drawn up by Chapelain, was accepted by the Cardinal who was reconciled to the mildness of the criticism only by the consideration, artfully presented by the Academy, that they must preserve a judicial tone in their review, if they desired it to be received with any respect by the people. The celebrated verdict thus rendered by the supreme court of culture in France was not satisfactory to any of the parties to the dispute. Richelieu and Scudéry had desired a far severer judgment; Corneille was justly indignant that it should be so severe. The Academy had clearly resorted to trimming. In their effort to mediate between the two sides, the learned judges censured here and praised there, sometimes with wisdom, often without. But though this verdict, which may be characterized as a mixture of fearfulness, feebleness and nascent good taste, falls far short of doing anything like justice to the beauties of Corneille's great creation, the poor, belabored Academicians should be given considerable credit for making even the stand that they did in behalf of literary merit and against the jealous anger of a despotic minister. Such a stand at such a time was a boon to literature.

The result of the contest was substantially a victory for Corneille. All France, as Balzac wrote to Scudéry, sided with the persecuted poet. In vain had his foes confederated against him ; a great nation, as one man, rose up to do him honor. CELA EST BEAU COMME LE CID became, in some parts of the country, a proverbial tribute to exalted excellence. Corneille decided, for prudential reasons, to make no reply to the strictures upon his piece ; the discomfited Scudéry with comic courtesy returned thanks to the Academy ; and Richelieu's resentment gradually cooled off. The pacification of the Cardinal was largely due to the kind offices of Mme. de Combalet, but for whom, according to Voltaire, Corneille would have been disgraced.

Thus was a very discreditable chapter in the history of French letters brought to a close. Across

11

the darkened scene, however, one golden gleam of purest light had fallen. While the other writers of the time were engaged in the vile work of detraction, the noble Rotrou, who stood head and shoulders above them all, remained Corneille's firm and faithful friend, giving his unstinted praise to the great poet's genius, and furnishing to the world a glorious example of lofty generosity. All honor to Jean Rotrou!

CHAPTER IV.

A CHARACTER STUDY: HORACE.

ABOUT two years had passed since the events recorded in our last chapter, when Corneille produced another magnificent masterpiece which appears pretty effectually to have stopped the mouths of his Lilliputian rivals. This time he sought his inspiration not in the legends of Spanish chivalry but in the glorious exploits, fabled, perhaps, yet true in spirit, of Rome's earliest heroes whose forms, as we look at them through the mist of tradition by which they are enveloped, seem grown to gigantic size. Taking for the subject of his drama the famous story of the combat between the three Curiatii and the three Horatii which has been preserved in Livy's amber Latin, our immortal poet composed a tragedy which must ever rank among the sublimest productions of the sublimest authors in French literature. Here Corneille was in his native element. No one was better fitted than he to present an ideal personification of that heroic patriotism which under the direction of far-seeing statesmanship reared a stupendous empire, bore Rome's eagles in triumph above the crimson tide of battle on a thousand famous fields, and compelled the proudest kings to fling down their diadems at her feet. The great poet's harp was attuned to just such themes as this. Though he had not proved his valor amid the "volleyed thunder" of contending armies, nor murdered his man in a duello, Corneille had, nevertheless, a heroic soul. Had this not been true he could never have composed either "Le Cid" or the martial drama which we are now about to examine. To describe the gallant deeds wrought by a hero's sword demands a hero's pen. The poet of warfare must be himself, potentially, a warrior.

With this much by way of introduction we begin at once our examination of the play. The title is "Horace," sometimes less correctly written "Les Horaces." The *dramatis personae* are Tulle, king of Rome; the old Horace, a Roman cavalier; Horace, his son; Curiace, a gentleman of Alba, and lover of Camille; Valère, a Roman cavalier, in love with Camille, but rejected by her; Sabine, wife of young Horace and sister of Curiace; Camille, lover of Curiace and sister of Horace; Julie, a Roman lady, confidant of Sabine and Camille; Flavian, an Alban soldier.

When the play opens Rome and Alba, inflamed by the lust of power, are engaged in fratricidal war. This day the stern arbitrament of battle is to decide which nation shall rule. In the first scene consisting of a dialogue between Sabine and Julie, the former laments her unhappy position, a prey as she is to clashing emotions.

"I am a Roman, alas!" she exclaims, "since Horace is a Roman;
I have received that title in receiving his hand;
But this tie would hold me as a chained slave,
If it hindered me from seeing in what places I was born.
Alba, where I began to breathe the day,
Alba, my dear country and my first love;
When between us and thee I see war opened,
I fear our victory as much as our defeat.
Rome, if thou complainest that that is to betray thee,
Make thyself enemies whom I can hate.
When I see from thy walls their army and ours,
My three brothers in one, and my husband in the other,
Can I form prayers, and without impiety,
Importune heaven for thy success?"

11*

This is a true cry of pain from a stricken heart. Continuing, Sabine says that she knows that Rome must enter upon a career of conquest. Thus only can she achieve the high destiny which the gods have marked out for her. Nor does Sabine condemn such ambitious projects.

" I would like already," she cries, "to see thy laurel-crowned
              troops
With victorious step pass over the Pyrenees.
Go, push on thy battalions even to the Orient;
Go plant thy standards upon the banks of the Rhine;
Make the pillars of Hercules tremble under thy steps,
But respect a city to which thou owest Romulus.
Ingrate, remember that from the blood of its kings
Thou hast thy name, thy walls and thy first laws.
Alba is thy origin; stop and reflect
That thou art plunging thy sword into the bosom of thy mother.
Direct elsewhere the efforts of thy triumphant arms;
Her joy will shine forth in the happiness of her children;
And allowing herself to be enraptured by maternal love,
Her prayers will be for thee, if thou art no longer against her."

Julie, recalling Sabine's seeming indifference heretofore to the fortunes of Alba, expresses herself as surprised at this sudden outbreak of emotion. Sabine replies that as long as the engagements occurring between the forces of the two nations were of too little moment seriously to affect the welfare of either, she did, indeed, boast that she was altogether Roman, but now that the fates of both cities hang trembling in opposite pans of the balance, now that all is staked upon the issue of one decisive battle, the smouldering embers of her love for Alba burst forth into flame.

" I am not for Alba," she says, " and I am no longer for Rome.
I fear for both in this last struggle,
And I will be of the side which fortune shall overthrow.
Impartial toward both until the victory,
I shall share in the woes without sharing in the glory ;
And in the midst of so many harsh rigors I keep
My tears for the vanquished and my hate for the victors."

" How very differently," remarks Julie, " Camille acts in our
      eyes !
Her brother is your husband, your brother is her lover :
But she sees with an eye very different from yours
Her blood in one army and her love in the other."

Julie then tells how much sorrow Camille had suffered on account of the minor combats which had previously taken place.

" But yesterday," continues the confidant, " when she knew that
      they had fixed a day,

And that at last a battle was going to be given,
A sudden joy shining upon her brow . . . . .

" Ah, Julie," interrupts Sabine, " how I fear a change so quick !
Yesterday in her fine humor she conversed with Valère ;
For this rival, doubtless, she abandons my brother ;
Her mind, moved by present objects,
Does not find an absent one worthy of love after two years."

Julie says that she can not explain Camille's conduct. Just at that juncture the latter approaches, and Sabine, bidding her talk to Julie, withdraws.

" How wrong she is," exclaims Camille, " to wish me to entertain you !
Does she think my grief less poignant than her own,
And that, more insensible to such great misfortunes,
I mingle fewer tears with my sad words?
My soul is alarmed with similar terrors ;
I shall lose like her in both armies.
I shall see my lover, my only wealth,
Die for his country or destroy mine ;
And this object of love become for my sorrow
Worthy of my sighs or worthy of my hate.
Alas ! "

Julie suggests that she discard Curiace and accept Valère. Camille rejects the idea with scorn. But

this exhibition of constancy does not slay the doubt
in Julie's mind.

" You disguise in vain," she exclaims, "a thing too clear :
I saw you yesterday converse with Valère,
And the gracious welcome which he received from you
Permits him to nourish a sweet enough hope."

Camille, hastening to explain away this charge
which makes her faithful heart wince with pain,
alludes to the happy hour when she and Curiace were
betrothed, tells how that very day scowling war arose
to thrust his bloody arm between them, speaks of their
agonized parting, and then continues thus :

" You have since seen the sorrows of my soul ;
You know what prayers my love has made for peace ;
And what tears I have shed at each event,
Now for my country, now for my lover.
At last my despair in these unending difficulties
Made me have recourse to the voice of oracles.
Hear whether the one which was given me yesterday
Was capable of assuring my distracted mind.
This Greek, so renowned, who for so many years
Has predicted our destinies at the foot of the Aventine,
He whom Apollo has never made speak falsely,
Promised me by these verses the end of my trials :
' Alba and Rome shall assume another aspect ;

Thy prayers are heard, they shall have peace,
And thou shalt be united to thy Curiace
Without any bad fortune ever separating thee from him?'
I derived from this oracle an entire assurance;
And, as the issue surpassed my hope,
I abandoned my soul to raptures
Which surpassed the transports of the happiest lovers.
Judge of their excess: I met Valère,
And, contrary to his custom, he could not displease me;
He spoke to me of love without wearying me;
I did not perceive that I was talking to him;
I could not show him scorn or coldness:
All that I saw seemed to me Curiace,
All that was said to me spoke to me of his love;
All that I said assured him of my affection.
The general combat is risked to-day;
I knew the tidings of it yesterday and I paid no attention to
        them:
My mind, charmed with the sweet thought of marriage and
        peace,
Rejected these ill-omened ideas.
Night has dissipated errors so enchanting;
A thousand frightful dreams, a thousand bloody images,
Or rather a thousand heaps of carnage and of horror,
Have snatched from me my joy and given me back my terror.
I have seen blood, dead men, and I have seen nothing connected;
A spectre, in appearing, suddenly took flight;
They effaced one another; and each illusion
Redoubled my fright by its incoherence."

Julie tries to reassure her, telling her that dreams go by contraries and that this grim battle which she dreads so much shall usher in smiling peace. Camille, however, is not to be comforted.

"Let the ill endure forever," she cries, "if it requires that
          remedy!
Whether Rome succumb in the contest or whether Alba be
          worsted,
Dear lover, no longer expect to be one day my husband;
Never, never shall that name be for a man
Who is either the conqueror or the slave of Rome."

As she utters these words she sees Curiace himself coming towards them, and exclaims:

"But what new person presents himself in these places?
Is it thou, Curiace? shall I believe my eyes?"
"Doubt thou not, Camille," he answers, "and behold again a
          man
Who is neither the conqueror nor the slave of Rome;
Cease to dread seeing my hands crimson
Under the shameful weight of fetters or with the blood of the
          Romans."

Camille, thinking that overcome by the power of his love for her he has deserted from the Alban army, declares that she has, nevertheless,

no word of reproach for his action. He quickly
undeceives her.

" I do not abandon the cause of my city,
I love still my honor while adoring Camille.
So long as the war lasted they saw me constantly
As good a citizen as true lover.
I reconciled Alba's quarrel with my love;
I sighed for you while fighting for her;
And if it were still necessary that one should come to blows,
I would fight for her while sighing for you."

He then explains that a cessation of hostilities has
permitted him to visit his beloved. She naturally
desires to know the reason for the truce, whereupon
he tells how, when the two hosts were drawn up
ready to charge, the Alban dictator, advancing before
his army, made an impassioned protest against this
internecine strife,

" In which the death of the vanquished enfeebles the victors,
And the most glorious triumph is watered with tears."

To put an end to the suicidal war he proposed that
each side choose three champions. These should do
battle for their respective states. The city whose

champions should be conquered must thenceforth train under the banners of the other.

"Thus," he concludes, "our two states shall make but one empire."

All joyfully agreed to this proposal. Each chieftain is now deliberating upon the choice of champions.

"O, gods," cries Camille, "how content these words make my soul!"

Curiace then finishes his report by telling her that her father has promised to bestow upon him her hand on the morrow.

"You will not become rebellious to his power?" asks the ardent lover.

"The duty of a daughter," Camille naïvely replies, "is in obedience."

Thus at the close of the first act the angel of peace for a time spreads her snowy wings above the rival armies. But soon, alas! her gentle soul is to be startled into flight by the clang of gleaming swords and the sight of flowing blood.

12

Act second commences with a scene between
Curiace and Horace. They have just learned that
Rome has chosen the three Horaces to fight for her.
Curiace after speaking of the high honor thus bestowed
upon the young heroes, an honor which, had it been
divided, might, he thinks, have covered three distinct
families with glory, goes on to say that, while he par-
ticipates as much as he can in the high distinction of
his brothers-in-law, he is filled with apprehension
for Alba.

"Since you fight," he declares, " her defeat is assured;
In causing you to be named, fate has sworn it.
I see but too clearly her baleful designs in this choice,
And I count myself already for one of your subjects."

" Whatever may be the designs of envious fate," answers Horace,
" I do not count myself for one of your subjects.
Rome has overestimated my worth; but my delighted soul
Will fulfil her expectation or renounce life.
He who wills to die or conquer is rarely conquered;
This noble despair perishes with difficulty.
Be that as it may, Rome shall never be subject
Unless my last gasps assure my defeat."

" Alas!" cries Curiace, " it is just here that I ought to be pitied.
What my country desires, my friendship fears.
Dire extremity, to see Alba enslaved,

Or her victory at the price of a life so dear;
Dire extremity, that the only boon to which her desires go out
Is purchased but by your last gasps!
What prayers can I form, and what happiness await!
On both sides I have tears to shed;
On both sides my hopes are deceived."

"What!" replies Horace, astonished, "What! you would weep
        for me dying for my country!
For a noble heart this death has charms,
The glory which follows it permits not tears.
And I would receive it and bless my fate,
If Rome and all the state lost less in my death."

Now ensues a scene which must thrill the most
stoical spectator. While Horace and Curiace are
still talking, Flavian appears bearing a message for
the latter. Let us listen to the dialogue that follows.

Curiace.

Has Alba made the choice of three warriors?

Flavian.

I come to apprise you of it.

Curiace.

Well, who are the three?

Flavian.

Your two brothers and you.

Curiace.

Who?

Flavian.

You and your two brothers.
But why this sad brow and these stern looks?
Does this choice displease you?

Curiace.

No, but it surprises me;
I esteemed myself of too little worth for an honor so great.

Flavian.

Shall I tell the dictator, whose order sends me hither,
That you receive it with so little joy?
This gloomy and cold reception surprises me in my turn.

Curiace.

Tell him that friendship, marriage ties and love
Will not be able to hinder the three Curiaces
From serving their country against the three Horaces.

Flavian.

Against them! Ah! that is to tell me much in a few words.

Curiace.

Take him my answer and leave us in repose.

After Flavian's withdrawal, Horace and Curiace, doomed, as they now know to contest against each other in mortal combat, discuss their dreadful situation. Here the poet's art is entitled to high praise. With fine effect he sets in sharp contrast the characters of the two young warriors.

Horace, heedless of the cries of affection, a stranger to fear, thoroughly possessed by the one thought of his duty to his country, is a type, somewhat exaggerated, of the stern, unyielding nation of soldiers who wrought and fought for Rome

" In the brave days of old."

" To combat an enemy," says he, " for the safety of all,
And against an unknown foe to expose oneself alone to the blows,
Is the ordinary effect of a common-place courage :
A thousand have already done it, a thousand could do it ;
To die for the country is so acceptable a lot,
That crowds would court so glorious a death :
But to be willing to sacrifice to the state what one loves,
To engage in a combat against another self,
To attack an enemy who takes for a defender
The brother of a wife and the lover of a sister,

12*

And, breaking all these ties, to arm oneself for the fatherland
Against blood which one would fain ransom with his life;
Such a courage belongs only to us."

Curiace is much nearer the ideal hero. Not less
patriotic, not less brave than Horace, the Alban is
far more intellectual, far more humane.

" I see," he says, sadly, " that your honor demands all my blood,
That all mine consists in piercing your breast;
That, about to espouse the sister, I must kill the brother;
And that for my country I have a lot so contrary.
While to my duty I hasten without terror,
My heart is shocked and I tremble with horror;
I pity myself and cast an envious eye
On those whose life our war has consumed,
Without the desire, however, of being able to retreat.
This sad and proud honor agitates me without unsettling me:
I love what it gives me, and I regret what it takes away;
And if Rome demands a higher courage,
I return thanks to the gods that I am not a Roman,
In order to preserve still some humanity."

The feelings of Horace are far different.

" Rome has chosen my arm," he cries, " I consider nothing,
With an alacrity as full and sincere
As that with which I espoused the sister, I will fight the brother;
And, finally, to cut short this useless talk,
Alba has named you, I know you no longer."

The reply of Curiace is admirable.

" I know you still," he says, " and it is that which kills me."

A moment later the stricken Camille joins them. Horace, bidding her bear up bravely in her grief, urges her in case he should be slain by Curiace, not on that account to steel her heart against her lover.

"Accomplish the marriage," says the just, if brutish brother,
        "as if I were living."
" But," he adds, " if this sword also cuts short his life,
Give to my victory a similar treatment ;
Reproach me not with the death of your lover.
Your tears are going to flow and your heart to ache ;
Consume with him all this weakness,
Quarrel with heaven and earth and curse fate ;
But after the combat think no more of the dead."

With these ominous words, which are the distant rumbling of a coming storm, Horace goes to seek Sabine and leaves the two lovers alone together.

Standing upon the very brink of the awful chasm of despair, their cheeks blanch, and their young hearts sicken and sink within them as they look down into its dreadful depths, where death sits grinning on his gory throne. " Wilt thou go, Curiace?"

questions Camille. His soul is bursting with volcanic grief. But he will do his duty, nevertheless. With tears in every tone he answers.

> "I pity you, I pity myself; but I must go."

Camille's entreaties are all in vain.

> "No," he cries, "No, Alba, after the honor which I have received
>   from thee,
> Thou shalt neither succumb nor conquer save by me;
> Thou hast entrusted to me thy fate, I will render thee a good
>   account of it,
> And will live without reproach, or perish without shame:"

> "What!" says Camille, "thou wilt not see that thou dost thus
>   betray me?"

Grandly he answers:

> "Before belonging to thee, I belong to my country."

The painful interview of the lovers is interrupted a few moments after this by the arrival of Horace and Sabine. We need not dwell upon the turgid rhetoric of the rather superfluous scene which follows. In it Sabine, phrensied with bitter woe, urges that either her husband or her brother take her life, and

so create a legitimate cause for their fatal strife.
Or, if this course be derogatory to their glory, she
begs them to pour out her blood as the initiatory
libation of their awful sacrifice to the Moloch of
savage patriotism. Should they not grant her request,
she will throw herself between their hurtling swords
upon the field of battle and perish thus. Her words,
while they wring the hearts of the warriors, can not
make them swerve from their duty.

The elder Horace now appears for the first time.

" What is this, my children," he demands, " do you listen to
        your love,
And do you still waste time with women ?
Ready to shed blood, do you regard tears ?
Flee and let them deplore their misfortunes.
Their plaints have too much art and tenderness for you :
They will make you share at length their weakness,
And it is only by fleeing that one parries such blows."

At this the women withdraw, Sabine exclaiming
as she departs,

" Tigers, go fight ; and for us, let us go die."

Young Horace then requests his father to watch
over Sabine and Camille and above all to keep

them from the scene of battle, lest by cries and tears they disturb the combat, and cause Rome's champions to be suspected of employing a cowardly artifice.

" I will take care of them," replies the noble old patriot,
"Go ; your brothers await you ;
Think only of the duties which your countries demand."

" What farewell shall I tell you ?" exclaims Curiace, "and by
what honoring phrase . . . . . "

" Ah ! touch not here my feelings ; " the heroic father cries in a speech admired by every critic for its peerless patriotism transfused with strong natural affection :

" My voice lacks words to encourage you ;
My heart does not form firm enough thoughts ;
I myself in this parting have tears in my eyes ;
Do your duty, and leave the rest to the gods."

So the dauntless warriors go forth to battle, while every heart in both armies beats high with excitement, and Atropos, the unavoidable, makes ready her glittering shears.

The marked difference in the merit of the first and second halves of the third act illustrates the unequal nature of Corneille's genius. In the one this bird of Jove is walking with folded wings upon the earth; in the other he soars amid the battling clouds and grasps the forked lightnings in his talons. The act begins with a tiresome monologue. "Sabine s'adresse sa pensée, la retourne, répète ce qu' elle a dit, oppose parole à parole."[1] She tries to extract some sips of honey even from sorrow's bitter herbs.

"Neither side can triumph,"[2] she muses, "save by the arms of my dear ones."

But this thought is soon succeeded by its obverse, and she says with hopeless sadness,

"Neither side can triumph save by the death of my dear ones."

Julie now arrives with tidings from the field. She announces that the two armies, when they discovered that the three Horatii and the three Curiatii had been chosen as champions by their respective nations, indignantly refused to allow soldiers so closely bound together by family ties to be pitted against each other in deadly strife.

[1] Voltaire.   [2] Lit. "One can only triumph," &c.

In vain did the champions, fearing lest they might lose their high renown, protest against this interruption. The two armies were determined that so barbarous a combat should not take place. They loudly demanded either that other combatants be selected or else that a general battle be joined. In the midst of this uproar the Roman king proposed that the question whether the Horatii should fight the Curiatii be left to the decision of the gods whose will was to be sought at once in sacrifice. The two armies agreed to this and all are now awaiting the report of the haruspices.

Like the grateful drops of a gentle rain in summer upon a drooping flower fall these words of Julie upon Sabine's sad heart. Gladly she welcomes returning hope.

Camille, on the contrary, with whom in the next scene Sabine and Julie discuss the situation, finds in the news no physic for despair. After some moments of conversation Julie retires. The two sisters-in-law, thus left by themselves, enter into a debate as to whose condition is the more deplorable. Camille maintains that marriage looses the bonds of birth ; that one's husband is incomparably dearer than one's brothers; and that Sabine, therefore, has only the death of Horace to dread.

Very much more harrowing, Camille thinks, is her own position. Curiace, the lover whom she was just about to marry, is less to her than a husband and not less than a brother. Her heart is thus convulsed with contrary feelings.

Sabine in reply says that love for a husband does not extinguish love for one's brothers; that the passion felt for a lover is after all more or less a matter of caprice; and that it is a crime to weigh such an attachment against the affection to which by nature's law one's brothers are entitled. Hence Sabine does not see why Camille can not offer up undivided prayers for her brothers' success.

Each of the ladies thus thinks her own burden the heavier. Their logical duel, so entirely out of place on such a solemn, such a tragic occasion, when every spectator, moreover, is eager to know what is going on in the field, is happily interrupted by the entrance of Camille's father, who announces that, agreeably to the will of the gods, the fatal combat is now in progress. Instantly our interest, chilled by the preceding scene, rises to fever heat. " Comme

13

l'arrivée du vieil Horace rend la vie au théâtre qui languissait!" exclaims Voltaire, "Quel moment et quelle noble simplicité!"

The grand old man pities the agony of the two women. His own soul is sorely tried. But his grief, he well understands, is not so hard to bear as theirs. The three Curiatii are indeed still very dear to him. He is not bound to them, however, by ties of love or blood. He can give his sympathy unreservedly to his own brave boys. He would have been rejoiced, he admits, had the gods forbidden this cruel combat and constrained Alba to choose other champions. The Horatii could then have conquered without shedding the blood of the Curiatii.

But "Dis aliter visum." The divine will must now be done. He therefore bids Sabine and Camille bear with pious faith and Roman fortitude the fearful calamity that has befallen them. As for himself, the fiery furnace of affliction only causes his golden character to glow with a brighter lustre. While he is striving to inspire them with his own heroic spirit Julie enters with news of the fight, and the following scene ensues.

The Elder Horace.

Do you come, Julie, to apprise us of the victory?

Julie.

Nay, rather of the baleful results of the combat.
Rome is the subject of Alba and your sons are defeated;
Of the three two are dead, her husband alone remains to you.

The Elder Horace.

O, truly baleful result of a sad combat!
Rome is the subject of Alba, and, to preserve her from it,
He has not employed even his last breath!
No, no, that is not true, they deceive you, Julie;
Rome is not subject, or my son is without life:
I know my blood better, he knows better his duty.

Julie.

A thousand from our ramparts have, like me, been able to see it.
He made himself admired so long as his brothers lived;
But, as he saw himself alone against three adversaries,
About to be surrounded by them, his flight saved him.

The Elder Horace.

And our betrayed soldiers have not dispatched him?
Have they given refuge in their ranks to this coward?

Julie.

I did not wish to see anything after this defeat.

Camille.

O, my brothers!

The Elder Horace.

Stop, weep not for them all;
Two enjoy a fate of which their father is jealous.
Let their tombs be covered with the noblest flowers;
The glory of their death has paid me for their loss.
This happiness has followed their unconquerable courage,
That they have seen Rome free as long as they lived,
And they will not have seen her obey any save her own
          prince,
Nor become the province of a neighboring state.
Weep for the other, weep for the irreparable disgrace
Which his shameful flight imprints upon our brow;
Weep for the dishonor of all our race,
And the eternal opprobrium which he leaves to the name of
          Horace.

Julie.

What did you wish that he should do against three?

The Elder Horace.

                              That he die,
Or that a fine despair should then succor him.
Had he only delayed his defeat one moment,
Rome would at least have been a little later subject;
He would have left my gray hairs with honor,
And that was a sufficiently worthy price for his life.

He is accountable to the fatherland for all his blood ;
Each drop spared has withered his glory ;
Each instant of his life, after this cowardly act,
Blazes abroad so much more my shame with his.
I shall speedily cut short his life, and my just wrath,
Using against an unworthy son the rights of a father,
Will well know how to display, in his punishment,
The signal disavowal of such an action.

Sabine.

Listen a little less to this noble heat,
And make us not utterly unhappy.

The Elder Horace.

Sabine, your heart is easily consoled ;
Our misfortunes thus far touch you feebly.
You have yet no part in our miseries ;
Heaven has saved to you your husband and your brothers.
If we are subject, 'tis to your country ;
Your brothers are conquerors when we are disappointed ;
And, seeing the high point to which their glory rises,
You regard very little what shame comes to us.
But your excessive love for this infamous husband
Will soon give you cause to sorrow like us.
Your tears are feeble defenses in his favor.
I call to witness the supreme powers of the great gods,
That before the end of this day, these hands, these very hands
Shall wash away in his blood the shame of the Romans.

13*

Sabine.

Let us follow him quickly, rage carries him away.
Gods! shall we always see such misfortunes?
Must we always dread greater ones,
And always fear the hand of our kindred?

Thus ends the third act. In the short initial scene of act fourth the elder Horace refuses to hearken to Camille's plea as she tries to calm his rage and to extenuate her brother's action. The poor old father maddened by the thought that son of his has proved himself a coward on the field of battle, betrayed the trust of Rome, and brought eternal disgrace upon the house of Horace, persists in his purpose to punish the culprit with death.

But now Valère appears in scene second with intelligence which puts an entirely new face upon matters. We will listen while he tells his story.

Valère.

Sent by the king to console a father,
And to testify to him . . . . .

The Elder Horace.

Take no trouble about it.
It is a solace of which I have not need;

And I prefer to see dead rather than covered with infamy
Those whom a hostile hand has just taken away from me.
Both of them died for their country like men of honor;
It suffices me.

Valère.

But the other is a rare blessing;
He ought to hold the place of all three with you.

The Elder Horace.

Why did not the name of Horace die with him?

Valère.

You alone outrage him after what he has done.

The Elder Horace.

It is for me alone, also, to punish his crime.

Valère.

What crime find you in his brave conduct?

The Elder Horace.

What display of courage find you in his flight?

Valère.

Flight is glorious on this occasion.

The Elder Horace.

You redouble my shame and my confusion.
Verily, the example is rare and worthy of memory,
To find in flight a road to glory.

Valère.

What confusion, and what shame for you
To have produced a son who saves us all,
Who makes Rome triumph, and wins her an empire?
To what greater honors needs a father aspire?

The Elder Horace.

What honors, what triumph, and what empire in fine,
When Alba under her laws ranges our destiny?

Valère.

What say you here of Alba and of her victory?
Are you ignorant still of half of the story?

The Elder Horace.

I know that by his flight he has betrayed the state.

Valère.

Yes, if he had in fleeing ended the fight;
But one soon saw that he only fled as a man
Who knew how to make the best use of the advantage of Rome.

The Elder Horace.

What, Rome then triumphs!

Valère.

Learn, learn
The valor of this son whom you wrongfully condemn.
Left alone against three, but, as it chanced,

All three being wounded, and he only without wound,
Too feeble for them all, too strong for each one of them,
He well knows how to extricate himself from a strait so hazardous;
He flees to fight the better, and this prompt ruse
Skilfully divides three brothers whom it deceives.
Each one follows him with a step or more or less rapid,
According as he finds himself or more or less wounded
Their ardor is equal to pursue his flight;
But their various wounds separate their pursuit.
Horace, seeing them separated one from another,
Turns about, and already believes them half conquered.
He awaits the first, and it was your son-in-law.
The other, all indignant that he should have dared await him,
In vain in attacking him displays great courage;
The blood that he has lost abates his vigor.
Alba in her turn begins to fear a contrary fate,
She cries to the second to succor his brother:
He hastens and exhausts himself in useless efforts;
He finds on coming up to them that his brother is no more.

Camille.

Alas!

Valère.

All out of breath he takes, however, his place,
And soon doubles the victory of Horace.
His courage without strength is a feeble support;
Wishing to avenge his brother he falls near him.
The air resounds with the shouts which all raise to heaven,
Alba utters cries of anguish and the Romans cries of joy.

As our hero sees himself about to finish,
It is little for him to conquer, he wishes also to show defiance:
"I have just immolated two of them to the shades of my
      brothers;
Rome shall have the last of my three adversaries,
'Tis to her that I am going to immolate him,"
Said he; and straightway they see him fly thither.
The victory between these two was not uncertain;
The Alban pierced with wounds only drags himself along with
      difficulty;
And, like a victim at the steps of the altar,
He seemed to present his throat to the fatal stroke:
Also he receives it almost without defense,
And his death establishes the power of Rome.

The Elder Horace.

O, my son! O, my joy! O, honor of our time!
O, unhoped for succor of a tottering state!
Valor worthy of Rome and blood worthy of Horace!
Support of thy country and glory of thy race!
When shall I be able to stifle in thy embrace
The error from which I have formed such false sentiments?
When shall my love be able to bathe with tenderness
Thy victorious brow in tears of joy?

Valère after assuring the now exultant father
that he shall soon see his gallant son, and after
delivering the king's twofold message of condolence

and congratulation, then retires to tell his majesty what noble sentiments animate the old patriot and how ardently he is devoted to the royal service. So the scene closes.

If, with Voltaire, we find in its first twenty or twenty-five verses "un artifice trop visible, une méprise trop longtemps soutenue," this fault is quite forgotten in the charm of the remaining portion.

"What, Rome then triumphs!"—the dynamic of Roman history is contained in these patriotic words. Patriotism incarnate it is that speaks. In vain must even the transcendant genius of a Hannibal battle against a people nerved to high exploits by such a sentiment, nay, by such a passion as this.

Observe, too, Valère's description of the combat. How vigorous, how vivid, how thrilling! The style is not unworthy of an epic bard.

The next few pages of the play are much inferior. In scene third the elder Horace with a coarseness near akin to brutality tells Camille that she can easily repair the loss of her lover by choosing one of the young gallants of Rome.

Sabine's loss, the old man thinks, is far more grievous. To her, therefore, he goes with words of consolation, bidding his weeping daughter choke down her sorrow and receive her brother with a sister's welcome.

Camille, thus left alone, rebels against her father's heartless injunction, recapitulates the story of her woe, and deliberately reasons herself into a white-heat of rage. She will not greet the conqueror with hollow words of compliment; she will boldly display her grief; she will strive to provoke his wrath; she will be true to her dead lover.

When, therefore, in scene fifth young Horace comes to claim from her his meed of praise, she bids him receive her tears. Mistaking her meaning, he replies that there is now no need of tears as he has avenged the death of his brothers.

"But," cries Camille, "who will avenge for me that of a lover,
To make me forget his love in a moment?"

Horace.

What dost thou say, unhappy girl?

Camille.

O, my dear Curiace!

Horace.

O, unbearable audacity of an unworthy sister!
The name of a public enemy whom I have conquered
Is in thy mouth and the love of him in thy heart!
Thy criminal passion aspires to vengeance!
Thy mouth demands it and thy heart ardently desires it!
Follow less thy passion, rule better thy desires,
No more make me blush to hear thy sighs:
Thy love hereafter ought to be stifled;
Banish it from thy soul, and think of my trophies;
Let them henceforth be thy only theme.

Camille.

Give me then, barbarian, a heart like thine;
And, if thou desirest in short that I should open to thee my soul,
Give me back my Curiace, or let my love have vent:
My joy and my grief depended on his fate;
I adored him living, and I weep for him dead.
Seek no more thy sister where thou hast left her;
Thou seest in me only an offended lover,
Who following like a fury upon thy footsteps,
Wishes incessantly to reproach thee with his death.
Bloodthirsty tiger who forbiddest my tears,
Who wishest that in his death I should still find delight,
And that, lauding to the skies thy exploits,
I myself should kill him a second time!
May so many misfortunes accompany thy life,
That thou mayst fall to the point of envying me!

14

And mayst thou soon soil by some base deed
This glory so dear to thy brutality!

Horace.

O heaven! who ever saw such rage!
Believest thou then that I am insensible to insult,
That I suffer in my blood this mortal dishonor?
Love, love this death which makes our good fortune,
And prefer at least to the memory of one man
What thy birth owes to the interests of Rome.

Camille.

Rome, the one object of my resentment!
Rome, to whom thy arm has just immolated my lover!
Rome, who saw thee born and whom thy heart adores!
Rome, in short, whom I hate because she honors thee!
May all her neighbors in conspiracy together
Sap her foundations yet ill assured!
And, if all Italy is not enough,
May the East league with the West against her;
May a hundred peoples united from all the ends of the world
Pass over both mountains and seas to destroy her!
May she herself overturn her walls upon herself,
And tear her vitals with her own hands!
May the wrath of heaven, kindled by my vows,
Rain upon her a deluge of fire!
May I with my eyes see this thunderbolt fall upon her,
See her houses in ashes, and thy laurels in dust,

See the last Roman in his last gasp,
I be the sole cause of it, and die of pleasure !

Horace

(Taking his sword in his hand, and pursuing his sister who flees).

'Tis too much, my patience gives way to justice ;
Go pity in Orcus thy Curiace !

Camille (wounded, behind the scenes).

Ah ! traitor !

Horace (returning upon the stage).

Let whoever dares weep for an enemy of Rome
Thus receive a sudden punishment !

Frightful as this deed of Horace is, it is in keeping with the character of that she wolf's whelp as already delineated in previous scenes. The murder of Camille was foreboded by his earlier speeches. It is the true resultant of such a nature and such an environment. What but butchery could follow when an insensate savage drunk with blood, swollen with pride, and restrained by no single prompting of fraternal affection, met his phrensied sister, who in electric flashes of fiercest hate cursed both him and Rome for the slaughter of her lover?

Nor are these scorching imprecations, so famous in French literature, the magniloquent declamation of artificial wrath. They are the fulminations of real passion.

The two remaining scenes of this act are very feeble. In scene sixth Procule, a Roman soldier who has not appeared in the play heretofore and who will not appear hereafter, mildly reproves Horace for his dastardly deed, exclaiming

"You ought to have treated her with less rigor."

"Tell me not," answers Horace hotly, "that she is both my
       blood and my sister.
My father can no longer avow her for his daughter:
Who curses his country, renounces his family."

Procule has nothing more to say. He is a poor, pitiable simulacrum of a character, utterly without *raison d'être*. Yet, though he does nothing and says nothing to advance the action of the drama, he still "lags superfluous" on the stage during the next scene. The interlocutors in this are Sabine and Horace. The frantic woman seeks death at her husband's hands.

"Join Sabine to Camille," she cries, "and thy wife to thy sister;
Our crimes are alike as well as our miseries,
I sigh like her, and mourn my brothers."

But Horace does not drench his laurels in the
blood of a second murder. He even exhibits some
semblance of feeling.

"I love thee," he exclaims, "and I know the grief which
        oppresses thee,
Embrace my virtue to conquer thy feebleness."

Sabine, however, spurns such virtue as but another
name for inhumanity. Then, finding after strenuous
efforts that she can not provoke him into killing her,
she changes her tone and begs him for death as
for a blessing.

"Dear husband," she pleads, "dear author of the torment
        which oppresses me,
Listen to pity, if thy choler ceases;
Exercise one or the other, after such misfortunes,
To punish my weakness, or end my griefs:
I ask for death as a boon, or as a punishment."

Horace, remarking upon the great power of women
over the noblest souls and fearing the effect of his
14*

wife's words upon his virtue, now seeks safety in
flight. Sabine, after the withdrawal of the men,
laments her ill success, but determines to continue
her quest of death. With these desperate utterances,
the tone of which has now become tiresome, the
scene and the act close.

The last act opens with a scene between the elder
Horace and his son. The sorely afflicted father
utters not a word of sharp reproach. The killing
of Camille, he says, was perfectly just. But he is
grieved that his son should have brought shame
upon himself by that act.

" Her crime," the old patriot aptly says, " though frightful
            and worthy of death,
Was better unpunished than punished by thy arm."

The son confesses his error, admits his father's
right to inflict paternal justice therefor and urges
him to put him to death. The father, however,
evidently has no such purpose. He looks upon his
son, he says, in a different light from that.

At this moment king Tulle enters accompanied
by Valère and a troop of guards. The king, com-
mending the fortitude of the elder Horace in his

affliction, expresses the most heartfelt sympathy for him. Then Valère, who cuts but a sorry figure in the whole tragedy, demands justice against the murderer in a speech which, as Voltaire remarks, "resembles that of a lawyer who has prepared himself." It is quite in the style of a prosecutor.

We need give only a synopsis of the speech. In the first place, Valère declares that the safety of the people demands the death of the sororicide, since almost everybody in Rome is weeping for some dear friend who has fallen while fighting in the Alban ranks, and if Horace be allowed to kill people for displaying such grief, the lives of wellnigh all the city will be put in jeopardy. Next the orator with artful words emphasizes the shamefulness of the deed. Then he argues that the chief cause of Horace's victory over the three Curiatii was not his own prowess, but the favorable destiny of Rome, since the gods, abandoning him to ruin, have allowed him so soon to soil his glory. Valère then closes with another appeal for justice upon the criminal.

The king now bids young Horace defend himself. Of his speech, also, we give but the outline. He makes no defence. On the contrary, he simply expresses in courtly words his entire submission to the royal authority; refers to the improbability of his ever having another such opportunity to distinguish himself as that which was presented in his combat with the Curiatii; and finally shows not only his willingness but his eagerness to die now before his glory shall be dimmed by less brilliant deeds.

At the conclusion of Horace's speech Sabine appears upon the stage. Her grief is too studied to be affecting. She begs the king to put her to death instead of Horace, declaring that that will punish him far more than would the taking of his own life, since he lives in her. Such action on the part of the king, she says, will be to her a joyful release from her present woes.

Now the elder Horace speaks. Here, as ever, he is the ideal Roman. So eloquent, so powerful, so patriotic, is his speech that we must give it all.

"Sire," he says, "it is then for me to answer Valère.
My children conspire with him against a father;
All three wish to destroy me, and arm themselves without reason
Against the little blood which remains in my house.

(to Sabine)

You, who, by grief contrary to your duty,
Wish to leave a husband in order to rejoin your brothers,
Go rather consult their noble shades;
They are dead, but for Alba, and they hold themselves happy;
Since heaven willed that she should be subjugated,
If any feeling remains after life,
This misfortune seems less, and less rude its strokes,
Seeing that all the honor of it falls upon us;
All three will disavow the grief which affects you,
The tears of your eyes, the sighs of your mouth,
The horror which you display of a valorous husband.
Sabine, be their sister, follow your duty like them.

(to the King)

Against this dear husband Valère in vain grows incensed:
A first impulse was never a crime;
And praise is due in place of punishment,
When virtue causes the first impulse.
To love your enemies with idolatry,
To curse the fatherland with rage at their death,
To wish an infinite misfortune to the state,
That is what is called crime, and what he has punished.
The love of Rome alone has nerved his hand;
He would be innocent, if he had loved her less.
What have I said, Sire? he is innocent, and this paternal arm
Would already have punished him, if he were criminal;
I would have known better how to use the absolute power

Which the right of fatherhood gives me over him;
I love honor too much, Sire, and am not of a rank
To suffer either insult or crime in my blood.
On this point I wish no other witness than Valère;
He has seen what reception my wrath reserved for him
When ignorant still of the half of the combat,
I believed that his flight had betrayed the state.
Who makes him charge himself with the cares of my family?
Who makes him, in spite of me, wish to avenge my daughter?
And for what reason does he take
In her just death an interest which a father does not?
They fear lest, after his sister, he may slay others!
Sire, we have part in the shame of our own kin alone,
And, in whatever way another may act,
He who is not related to us does not make us blush.

(to Valère)

You can weep, Valère, and even before the eyes of Horace;
He is interested only in the crimes of his kindred:
He who is not of his blood can not offer an insult
To the immortal laurels which circle his brow.
Laurels, sacred branches that they wish to reduce to dust,
You that protect his head from the thunderbolt,
Will you abandon him to the infamous knife
Which makes the wicked fall under the hand of the executioner?
Romans, will you suffer that a man be slain
Without whom Rome to-day would cease to be Rome,
And that a Roman strive to stain the renown
Of a warrior to whom all owe such a glorious name?

Tell us, Valère, tell us, if you wish that he perish,
Where think you to choose a place for his punishment:
Will it be between these walls which thousands of voices
Still cause to resound with the noise of his exploits?
Will it be outside the walls in the midst of those places
Which are still seen to smoke with the blood of the Curiaces?
Between their three tombs and in the field of honor,
Witness of his valor and of our good fortune?
You would not know how to conceal his punishment from his
        victory:
In the walls, outside the walls, all speaks of his glory,
All opposes the efforts of your unjust love,
Which would stain so glorious a day with such good blood:
Alba will not be able to suffer such a sight,
And Rome by her tears will put too great an obstacle in the way.
You will anticipate them, Sire, and by a just decree
You will know how to conserve much better her interest.
What he has done for her he still can do;
He can guard her still from an adverse fate.
Sire, grant nothing to my feeble years:
Rome has to-day seen me the father of four children;
Three in this same day have died for her quarrel:
There rèmains to me one; preserve him for her;
Take not from her walls so powerful a support;
And permit me, in conclusion, to address myself to him.
Horace, believe not that the stupid populace
Is the absolute master of a truly solid renown.
Its tumultuous voice often enough makes a noise,
But a moment raises it, a moment destroys it;

And what it contributes to our renown
Is always in less than no time dissipated in smoke.
It is for kings, it is for the great, it is for minds well made,
To see valor perfect in its least effects;
It is from them alone that one receives true glory,
They alone assure the memory of true heroes.
Live always like an Horace; and always among them
Your name shall be great, illustrious, famous,
Although the opportunity, less lofty or less brilliant,
Should disappoint the unjust expectation of an ignorant
   populace.
Hate, then, no longer your life, and at least live for me,
And to serve again your country and your king.
Sire, I have said too much; but the affair concerns you;
And all Rome has spoken by my mouth.

What a superb speech this is! How the majesty of
the man's character informs every sentence! Nature
boasts no nobler brand of patriot than this.

The decision of Tulle is just what all expected it
to be. While acknowledging that young Horace
has committed a heinous crime against the laws of
the state, and that he deserves death therefor, the
king declares that the distinguished public services
of the culprit, the fact that he has saved his country
from slavery, and brought beneath her sceptre another
city, have raised him above the laws.

" Live," therefore, cries Tulle, " Live to serve the State."

The king closes his speech with a tender reference to Camille.

"I pity her," he says, "and in order to render to her rigorous
        fate
What her loving heart may wish,
Since in one same day the ardor of one same zeal
Ends the destiny of her lover and of her,
I desire one same day, witness of their two deaths,
To see their bodies enclosed in one same tomb."

Thus the play ends. In the first edition there was another scene in which Julie, pronouncing, alone, a monologue, apostrophizes Camille, speaks of the boundless happiness which heaven seemed to promise her through the oracle of the Greek priest mentioned in the first act, and calls attention to the perfect fulfilment of that oracle, though in a manner totally unexpected by them. This scene was, however, very properly omitted as superfluous in subsequent editions.

The glaring defect of the fifth act is that it is barren of action and consists solely of speeches. Corneille himself with that noble candor which

15

ever glistens brightly in his diadem of virtues
frankly confesses this. Speaking of that act he
says : " Il est tout en plaidoyers ; et ce n'est pas là
la place des harangues et des longs discours." It
is to be remembered, however, that while this scene
of oratory is a serious fault, the oratory in itself
considered is, as we have seen, of the noblest kind.
The effects of Corneille's legal training are here
quite evident. He had certainly learned the art
and the artifice of the French pleaders.

With the production of " Horace," whose profoundly conceived characters, thrilling interest and
massive eloquence, far outweigh all defects, the
formative period of the French drama may be said
to close. Chaos has now yielded to cosmos. The
potential mixture has crystallized into the regular
forms of the classic theatre. A mould of drama
has been established which, remaining unchanged
while blazing châteaux light up the midnight
darkness, while the streets of Paris blush crimson
at her children's crimes, and while all things save
literature are fused in the crucible of Revolution,
shall only be broken at last by the weird tooting of
Hernani's horn, when it calls Classicism to its death.

Henceforth the three unities are to dictate to poets and determine the outline of every drama, as three points determine a circle.

What are these unities, and how did they come to enthrall the theatre of France? In order to answer those questions intelligently we must take a rapid glance at the history of the serious drama of Greece which the French classicists claim to have imitated.

That drama, as has been said, grew out of the worship of Dionysus. The name tragedy, derived from τράγος, a goat and ᾠδή, a song, and signifying thus a goat-song, was probably chosen because of the fact that the performers of the primitive Dionysiac songs and dances, who were disguised as satyrs, were clothed in goat skins.

This explanation is not accepted by all. Some suppose that the term was adopted because a goat was sacrificed to Dionysus on such occasions, and still others because a goat was the prize offered.

However that may be, it is quite clear that the classic Greek tragedy was developed from the mournful dithyrambic odes which were designed to express the sufferings of Dionysus and were sung by a chorus of fifty men as they danced around the altar of the god.

The chorus was thus the embryon of the serious drama.

A great improvement was made when Thespis, in order to give rest to the chorus, introduced a single actor who added an epic element to the hitherto purely lyrical tragedy, engaged in dialogue with the leader of the chorus, and by the use of linen masks was able to represent the different characters of the piece.

Such was the serious drama when it passed into the hands of Aeschylus (525–456, B. C). That immortal master, the real father of Greek tragedy made further radical changes. He brought a second actor upon the stage, introduced painted scenes, provided for the actors more magnificent costumes and invented the needed auxiliary machinery. The dialogue now became the dominant feature, while the chorus was made subsidiary. Henceforth the evolution of the tragedy is but a process of elaboration, the most important improvement being the introduction by Sophocles of a third actor, which enabled the poet to add greater scope, variety and richness to his dialogue.

English readers will form an excellent conception of Greek tragedy in this, its most perfect form, from a study of Milton's magnificent play, "Samson Agonistes."

Another piece, also written in the Greek style, but far inferior to Milton's great poem is Swinburne's "Atalanta in Calydon." Both of these authors have succeeded in no small degree in reproducing Greek form. The classic spirit breathes from every page.

The tragedy of the Greeks, which was distinguished for its solemn majesty, its massive grandeur and its stately beauty—qualities largely owing, doubtless, to its religious origin and to the fact that the poet generally sought his subject in the mythology of his native land,—was simple in plot, but in the highest degree artistic in execution.

The action of the play from prologue to exode must be one closely forged chain of cause and effect. Every incident must be a tributary to one main stream flowing onward to the cataract of catastrophe. This oneness in the action produces in the spectator a oneness of interest.

15*

No considerable change of place was permissible in the play, nor did the time supposed to be occupied by the action often exceed one day. From these facts were deduced the three laws known as the unity of action, the unity of place and the unity of time, which have ruled the French theatre with despotic sway and which have been aptly stated by Boileau in the following famous lines:

> "Qu'en un lieu, qu'en un jour, un seul fait accompli
> Tienne jusqu'à la fin le théâtre rempli."

French poets and critics have very generally attributed those laws to Aristotle, though but little warrant can be shown for so doing. As a matter of fact that great philosopher speaks but briefly and somewhat indistinctly of the unity of action, never once mentions the unity of place and in regard to the unity of time merely makes the remark that tragedy "seeks as far as possible to circumscribe itself within one revolution of the sun, or to exceed this very little." The three unities can not be greatly buttressed, therefore, by the authority of Aristotle.

Were we ignorant of the literary history of France, did we not know how classic literature was idolized after the revival of learning, we should be amazed at seeing these rules established as the inviolable laws of the French stage. But it is evident that the explanation of this voluntary servitude is to be found in that blind worship of the past which was for so long prevalent in France. It was simply another example of classicism carried to excess.

Unity of action, indeed, every perfect play must have. But the unity of place and the unity of time, except so far as these are from the nature of things bound up with the unity of action, are needless chains which hamper the movements and rasp the bones of genius.

The character of the Greek representations, and especially the fact that they were continuous, made such restrictions eminently proper in Greece, although even there they were sometimes not observed.

But in modern times, when the curtain falls at the end of every act, and when each of these five divisions may be regarded as a photograph of one phase of a comprehensive action, no sufficient reason can be adduced for wearing these manacles.

CHAPTER V.

A TRAGEDY OF THE GOLDEN AGE OF ROME: CINNA.

IN the plays of Corneille we have a series of stereopticon views which picture in vivid colors the successive stages of the historic development of the Roman people from the time when the gray light of dawning history first falls upon their insignificant city of thatched huts, through the splendors of the empire, when these huts had given place to marble palaces with sculptured columns and mosaic pavements, when all roads led to Rome, and when she was the great heart of the civilized world, down to the time when the cancer of corruption was doing within her its work of death.

Recognizing this fact, M. Ernest Desjardins entitles his work on our author, "Le Grand Corneille, Historien." Upon one such historic picture we have already looked. We have seen with what verve

and vigor the famous dramatist has portrayed in
" Horace " the hardy patriots of legendary times.

We are now to gaze on very different scenes.
Roman freedom lies dead, slain by the same sword-
stroke that beheaded Cicero; the government, though
republican in form, is imperial in fact; with marvel-
ous skill a sagacious despot is acting beneath a painted
mask his rôle of patron, protector and *pater patriœ;*
the golden chains which bind the people hang so
loosely about their limbs, glitter so brightly in the
sunlight of general prosperity, and clink so musi-
cally together link on link that the thoughtless
citizens have forgotten that they are slaves; the
upper classes are reveling in wealth, luxury and
fashion; three civilizations—the Oriental, the Greek
and the Latin—have poured their treasure together
into the vast smelting-pot of the cosmopolitan city;
literature's boughs are laden with a beautiful fruitage; culture is being widely diffused; the army on
whose firm shoulders rests the whole fabric of the
empire holds a conquered world in subjection; stal-
wart opposition to despotism there is none; but in
spite of the conciliatory policy of the artful Octavius,
in spite of bribery and intrigue and force, in spite

of lictors and legions, in spite of the apathy of the
people and the cowardice of the nobles, there are
some to whom the memory of the old republic still
is sacred and in whose heart of hearts the hatred of
tyranny burns like a consuming fire, pent up, indeed,
but liable at any moment to burst forth in fury.

Such is the setting of circumstance in which Corneille places his next tragedy, "Cinna," a play
which appeared in 1639, and which is thought by
not a few critics to be its author's grandest creation.
The *dramatis personæ* are Auguste, Emperor of
Rome; Livie, the Empress; Cinna, son of a daughter of Pompey; Maxime, a young man of rank;
Émilie, daughter of C. Soranius, tutor of Auguste
and proscribed by him during the triumvirate;
Fulvie, confidant of Émilie; and Polyclète, Évandre and Euphorbe, freedmen, respectively of Auguste,
Cinna and Maxime.   The play opens with a monologue by Émilie, composed in that grand style for
which Corneille is famous and which, though to
Americans it may at times seem somewhat turgid,
is yet admirably suited to the portraiture of the
grandeur of Roman character, to the expansion of
the poet's own sublime soul, and to the taste of the

people that he wrote for—a people to whom, as to
their Celtic forefathers, oratory is an instinct and
the pomp of splendid declamation next in esteem to
" battle's magnificently stern array."

Émilie, though she is daily the recipient of undeniable marks of the Emperor's most distinguished
favor, nevertheless secretly hates him as her father's
murderer and passionately desires his destruction.
She has, therefore, made it a necessary condition to
her marrying her lover, Cinna, that he, in spite of
his own heavy obligations to Auguste shall form
and carry to a successful issue a conspiracy of dis-
contented nobles against his life. Cinna has accepted
her hard terms. Now, however, when the mine is
about to be sprung, even this implacable woman,
this veritable Nemesis, whose heart " *robur et aes
triplex*" encase, begins to feel anxious fears for her
lover's safety, finds two emotions battling in her
soul, and for a moment pauses to consider whether
she shall even for vengeance risk the object of her
passion. Her soliloquy shows well her painful
position. We translate the scene entire.

Émilie.

Impatient desires for an illustrious revenge,
Whose birth my father's death has formed,

Impetuous children of my wrath,
Which my deluded grief blindly embraces,
You assume too powerful a sway over my soul:
Permit me for few moments to breathe,
And to consider, in the state in which I am,
Both what I hazard and what I aim at.
When I behold Auguste in the midst of his glory,
And when you reproach my sad memory with the fact
That my father, massacred by his very hand,
Forms the first step of the throne on which I see him,
When you present to me this bloody image,
The cause of my hate and the effect of his rage,
I abandon myself entirely to your ardent transports,
And believe that for one death I owe him a thousand deaths.
In the midst, however, of a fury so just,
I love Cinna still more than I hate Auguste,
And I feel this boiling emotion grow cool,
When to follow it, I must expose my lover.
Yes, Cinna, against myself I myself become angered,
When I think of the perils into which I thrust thee.
Although in my service you fear nothing,
To demand of thee blood, is to expose thine own:
From so high a place one casts not down heads
Without drawing upon oneself a thousand tempests;
The issue of it is doubtful, the peril certain:
A faithless friend may betray thy design;
The plan ill-arranged, the occasion ill chosen,
May overturn the enterprise upon its author;
Direct upon thee the blows with which thou wishest to strike him;

In his ruin, even, he may envelop thee;
And whatever thy love may execute in my behalf,
He may, in falling, crush thee under his fall.
Ah! cease to run upon this deadly peril;
To destroy thyself in avenging me, is not to avenge me.
A heart is too cruel when it finds any delights
In pleasures which the bitterness of tears corrupts;
And one should put in the rank of the severest misfortunes
An enemy's death which costs so many tears.

But can one shed any when one avenges a father?
Is there any loss at that price which does not seem light?
And when his assassin falls under our effort
Ought one to consider what his death costs?
Cease, vain fears, cease, cowardly affection,
To throw into my heart your unworthy weakness;
And thou who dost produce them by thy superfluous cares
Love, serve my duty, and combat it no longer!
To yield to it is thy glory, and to conquer it thy shame.
Show thyself noble, permitting that it overcome thee:
The more thou shalt give it, the more it is going to give thee,
And it will only triumph in order to crown thee.

After this passionate monologue comes a conversation between Émilie and Fulvie. " Ce n'est qu'une scène avec une confidante," says Voltaire, " et elle est sublime." Émilie announces her determination to persist to the bitter end in her plot

16

against the Emperor's life, whatever may be the consequences to Cinna. It is to no avail that Fulvie seeks to turn her from her tragic purpose. No tigress could be more ferocious than is she. The confidant refers to the Emperor's uniform kindness to her mistress and his evident affection for her. But Émilie will not hear to the argument.

" All this favor," she cries, "does not give me back my father ;
And, however people may consider me,
Abounding in riches or powerful in influence,
I remain always the daughter of a proscript.
Benefactions do not always do what you think ;
From an odious hand they are equivalent to offences :
The more of them we lavish on him who may hate us,
The more arms we give to him who wishes to betray us.
He bestows favors on me each day without changing my heart ;
I am what I was, and I am more powerful.
And with the same presents which he pours into my hands
I buy the minds of the Romans against him ;
I would receive from him the place of Livie
As a surer means of making an attempt upon his life.
For one who avenges a father there are no crimes,
And to yield to favors is to sell one's blood."

In such words, bursting like volcanic fire from her lips, does the orphan girl pour forth her molten

soul. Fulvie then urges her, while hating Auguste
as much as she pleases in secret, to leave the desperate
task of assassinating him to the hundreds of other
Romans who had been as deeply wronged as she,
and who doubtless only await a favorable opportunity to strike. This course, however, Émilie
utterly condemns. If Auguste should fall thus,
pierced by a dagger in a hand which she had
not nerved to action, her father would not be
avenged. No, she must herself be the real cause
of the Emperor's death. It would be base and
cowardly to shirk her duty. Seeing the futility
of all other arguments, Fulvie now advances her
strongest one. She speaks of the imminent peril
which Cinna must incur in executing the proposed
plot.

" Be not blind," she exclaims, " when his death is visible."
" Ah, thou knowest how to strike me where I am sensitive,
        cries Émilie;
" When I think of the dangers which I make him run,
The fear of his death makes me already die;
My mind in disorder is opposed to itself;
I wish and I do not wish, I am enraged and I dare not;
And my duty confused, languishing, astounded,
Yields to the rebellions of my mutinous heart."

Yet, despite all of passion's powerful pleading, she is still firmly resolved to do what she believes to be her duty. The tyrant's blood must be offered as a sacrifice to the shade of her father. If her lover be slain in the attempt to carry out her behest, she will die after him.

Just then Cinna comes upon the stage. He is fresh from a meeting of the band of conspirators. Émilie eagerly and anxiously asks in what frame of mind he found them—whether or not they were dismayed at the prospect of their desperate attempt to throttle despotism. Cinna is all aflame with enthusiasm.

" Never," he answers, " did an enterprise conceived against a
        tyrant
Permit one to hope so glorious an issue :
Never did people swear a tyrant's death with such ardor ;
And never were conspirators better agreed ;
All appear impelled to this project with so much alacrity
That they seem, like me, to serve a mistress ;
And all display a wrath so intense
That they all seem, like you, to avenge a father."

Émilie.

I had well foreseen that for such a work
Cinna would know how to choose men of courage,

And would not entrust to bad hands
The fate of Émilie and that of the Romans.

Cinna.

Would to the gods that you yourself had seen with what zeal
This band undertake an enterprise so noble!
At the mere name of Cæsar, of Auguste and of emperor,
You would have seen their eyes flame up with fury,
And in the same instant, by an opposite effect,
Their brow grow pale with horror and flush with rage.
"Friends," said I to them, "this is the happy day
Which is to consummate at last our noble designs;
Heaven has put the fate of Rome in our hands,
And her safety depends on the destruction of one man,
If one owes the name of man to him who has nothing human,
To this tiger thirsting for all the Roman blood.
How many intrigues has he formed to shed it!
How many times has he changed parties and leagues,
Now the friend of Antony and now his enemy,
And never insolent nor cruel by halves!"
There by a long recital of all the woes
Which our fathers suffered during our infancy,
Reviving their hate with their recollection,
I redouble in their hearts the ardor of punishing him;
I paint for them pictures of those sad battles
In which Rome by her own hands tore her own vitals,
In which the eagle struck down the eagle, and on each side
Our legions armed themselves against their liberty;
In which the best soldiers and the bravest chief

16*

Made it all their glory to become slaves;
In which to better assure the shame of their own fetters
All wished to attach the universe to their chain;
And the execrable honor of giving it a master
Making all love the infamous name of traitor,
Romans against Romans, kinsmen against kinsmen,
Fought only for the choice of tyrants.
I add to these pictures the frightful painting
Of their union, impious, dreadful, relentless,
Deadly to people of worth, to the rich, to the senate;
And, to say all, in short, of their triumvirate:
But I find not colors black enough
To represent their tragic records.
I paint them revelling with emulation in murder,
All Rome drowned in the blood of her children:
Some assassinated in the public squares,
Others in the midst of their household gods;
The wicked encouraged to crime by rewards,
The husband butchered by his wife in his bed;
The son all dripping with the slaughter of the father,
And, with his head in his hand, demanding his recompense;
Without being able to express by so many horrible touches
More than an imperfect sketch of their bloody peace.
Shall I tell you the names of those great personages
Whose death I painted to embitter their hearts,
Of those famous proscripts, those human demi-gods,
Who have been sacrificed even upon the altars?
But could I tell you to what impatience,
To what shudders, to what violence,

These infamous murders, though ill-portrayed,
Moved the minds of all our conspirators?
I did not lose time, and seeing their wrath
At the point of fearing nothing, in a state to do everything,
I add in a few words: "All these cruelties,
The loss of our properties and of our liberties,
The devastation of the fields, the pillage of the cities,
And the proscriptions, and the civil wars
Are the bloody steps which Auguste has chosen
To rise to the throne and give us laws.
But we can change a destiny so dire,
Since of three tyrants he is the only one who remains to us,
And since, just for once, he has deprived himself of support,
Destroying, in order to reign alone, two wicked men like him-
　　　self:
He being dead, we have no avenger to fear nor master to serve;
With liberty Rome will revive;
And we shall merit the name of true Romans,
If the yoke which weighs her down is broken by our hands.
Let us take the opportunity while it is propitious:
To-morrow at the Capitol he makes a sacrifice;
Let him be the victim, and let us do in these places
Justice to all the world in the sight of the gods:
There, he has hardly more than our band for his suite;
It is from my hand that he takes both the incense and the cup;
And I desire this same hand, for signal,
To give him, instead of incense, a blow with a poniard in his
　　　breast.
Thus the victim stricken with a mortal wound

Will make it appear whether I am of the blood of the great
       Pompey;
Make it appear, after me, whether you remember
The illustrious ancestors from whom you are descended."
Scarcely had I finished when each one renews
By a noble oath the vow to be faithful:
The opportunity pleases them; but each desires for himself
The honor of the first blow which I chose for myself.
Reason rules at last the ardor which transports them:
Maxime and one half make sure of the door;
The other half follow me and are to surround him,
Ready at the least signal which I shall give.
That is the point to which we have arrived in the matter,
       beautiful Émilie.
To-morrow I await the hatred or the favor of men,
The name of parricide or of liberator;
Cæsar, that of prince or usurper.
On the issue which they obtain against tyranny
Depends either our glory or our ignominy;
And the people, inconsistent with regard to tyrants,
If they detest them when dead, adore them while living.
As for me, whether heaven be hard or propitious to me,
Whether it lift me to glory or deliver me to punishment,
Whether Rome declare herself either for or against us,
Dying to serve you, all will seem sweet to me."

Even in our bald, literal translation the powerful
eloquence of this passage will, we hope, be felt by
every reader. But when one studies the original

French with its vivid color, its nervous energy and its sonorous versification, one sees how truly Corneille deserves the title " *Grand*," and how sublime are those sheer heights to which he sometimes soars. Every line vibrates under the breath of intense emotion. The spectator is swept away by the rushing flood of Cinna's declamation. Our hearts are fired by his fervid words of patriotism; we long to see Rome rend her fetters; we loathe the bloody crimes of Auguste; we tremble at the peril that threatens to engulf the two lovers; we are profoundly interested in the outcome of this conspiracy, fraught with such momentous consequences to them and to the state. Especially is it to be noted, also, that both in sentiment and in style the scene is intensely Roman.

But we must return to the story. Émilie, well pleased with her lover's ardent devotion, confirms him in his daring and dangerous purpose, urging him, however, not to expose his life unnecessarily. Their conversation is now interrupted by the arrival of the freedman Évandre, who tells Cinna that Auguste commands both him and Maxime to repair immediately to his presence. The cheeks of the lovers blanch at this announcement.   Has the Emperor discovered the conspiracy?   If not, why does he send for the two leaders?

Even Émilie's stout heart grows faint within her at the thought of losing her lover, and she begs him abandon the plot and flee from the wrath of Auguste.   Cinna is much more calm.   He revives the courage of his terrified mistress, telling her that perhaps this is a false alarm, and that, even if it prove true, his evident duty as a man of honor is to meet death fearlessly in her quarrel, a duty which he will gladly and proudly perform.   Émilie bids him, then, go forth in this bold spirit.

"If you must die," she cries, "die like a Roman citizen,
And by a noble death crown a noble design."

She indicates in conclusion that she is determined not to survive him.   Cinna, however, would dissuade her from such a course, informing her that her connection with the conspiracy is unknown save to their faithful confidants and urging her to live to avenge him as well as her father.   Émilie then says that she will seek the Empress and, in case the plot is discovered, will employ both the influence of Livie and her own in behalf of her lover. But she reiterates her determination to end her life, too, if he must perish.

" For my sake," pleads Cinna, " be less cruel to yourself."
" Go," she answers, "and only remember that I love you."

With these affectionate words the act closes. When the curtain rises again, we behold Auguste surrounded by a troop of courtiers among whom are Cinna and Maxime. The Emperor bids all retire save the two chiefs of the conspiracy. Then, when his command has been obeyed, he addresses them in the following words :

" This absolute empire over land and sea,
This sovereign power which I have over all the world,
This grandeur without limit and this illustrious rank
Which cost me formerly so much pain and blood,
In short all in my high fortune
Which the importunate presence of a flattering courtier
            adores,
Is only beauties whose splendor dazzles,
And which one ceases to love as soon as one enjoys them.
Ambition displeases when it is satiated,
And its ardor is followed by a contrary ardor ;
And as our mind, even till our last sigh,

Always puts forth some desire toward some object,
It turns back upon itself, having nothing else to lay hold on,
And, having risen to the summit, it aspires to descend.
I wished for the empire and I have obtained it;
But when I wished for it I did not know it:
In its possession I have found, as its only charms,
Frightful cares, alarms eternal,
A thousand secret enemies, death at every turn,
No pleasure without uneasiness, and never any rest."

As the crown has thus grown heavy upon his brow and the sweets of power have cloyed to his taste, the Emperor is debating in his own mind the expediency of abdicating. Upon this momentous question he desires the advice of Cinna and Maxime. It is for this that he has summoned them into his presence. He bids them speak their minds with perfect freedom and frankness.

"Consider not," he says, "this supreme grandeur,
Hateful to the Romans, and burdensome to myself;
Treat me as friend, not as sovereign;
Rome, Auguste, the state—all is in your hand:
You shall put Europe, and Asia, and Africa,
Under the laws of a monarch or of a republic;
Your advice is my rule, and by virtue of that alone
I will be Emperor or private citizen."

What a thrilling situation is this! The master of a mighty empire, the great ruler at whose word three continents tremble, has chosen as the arbiters of his destiny the two conspirators who have sworn to dye their daggers upon the morrow in his blood. Cinna strongly advises the Emperor not to resign his power.

"One does not renounce legitimate grandeur," says the con-
        spirator;
"One keeps without remorse what one acquires without crimes;
And the nobler, grander, more exquisite the fortune one sur-
        renders,
The worse he who dares give it up, deems it to have been
        acquired.
Imprint not, my lord, this shameful stamp
Upon those rare virtues which have made you monarch;
You are so justly, and it is without crime
That you have changed the form of the state.
Rome is under your laws by the right of war,
Which has put all the earth un der the laws of Rome;
Your arms have conquered her, and all conquerors
Are not tyrants because they are usurpers;
When they have reduced provinces under their laws,
Governing justly, they make themselves just princes;
That is what Cæsar did; you must to-day
Condemn his memory, or do as he did.

17

If supreme power is censured by Auguste,
Cæsar was a tyrant, and his assassination was just,
And you owe to the gods an account for all the blood
With which you have avenged him to rise to his rank.
Fear not, my lord, his sad fate;
A more powerful genius watches over your years:
Ten times have they attempted your life without effect,
And the one who wished to destroy him did it the same instant.
They plot enough, but no one executes;
There are assassins, but there is no Brutus:
In fine, if you must expect such a catastrophe,
It is glorious to die master of the world."

It is, of course, quite apparent to the spectator why Cinna speaks thus. If Auguste lays down his sceptre, all Rome will join in one universal anthem of praise, the conspiracy will vanish like a gruesome vision of the night, and Émilie will fail of her revenge. All this flashes through Cinna's mind, his love conquers his patriotism, and he strives by flattering words to lure Auguste on to a bloody death.

Very different is the course of Maxime. He admits that Auguste has the right to rule as monarch of Rome, but denies that abdication would be in any sense a confession that he had himself obtained

his power unjustly or a reflection upon the legitimacy
of Cæsar's reign.   Maxime then continues thus:

" Rome is yours, my lord, the empire is your property;
Everyone can dispose of his own in liberty;
He can at his choice keep it or part with it:
Were Cinna's view correct, you alone could not do what the
        herd can,
And would have become, for having conquered all,
The slave of the glories to which you have risen!
Possess them, my lord, without their possessing you;
Far from leading you captive, suffer that they obey you;
And boldly make it known in short to all
That all that those glories embrace is beneath you.
Your Rome formerly gave you birth;
You wish to give her your supreme power;
And Cinna imputes to you as a capital crime
Liberality towards your native land!
He calls the love of country remorse!
Glory is then tarnished by lofty virtue,
And this is only an object worthy of our scorn,
If infamy is the reward of its perfect consummation.
I will indeed confess that an action so noble
Gives to Rome much more than you hold from her;
But does one commit a crime unworthy of pardon,
When his gratitude is above the gift?
Follow, my lord, follow, heaven which inspires you:
Your glory redoubles when you scorn imperial power;

And you will be famous among posterity,
Less for having conquered than for having resigned it.
Good fortune may lead you to supreme glory,
But to renounce it virtue itself is needed;
And few noble souls, after a sceptre has been won,
Go so far as to disdain the pleasure of ruling.
Consider moreover that you reign in Rome,
Where, whatsoever title your court may give you,
Monarchy is hated; and the name of emperor,
Concealing that of king, causes not less horror.
They regard as a tyrant whoever makes himself their master;
Him who serves him as a slave, and him who loves him as a
        traitor.
He who endures him has a heart cowardly, weak, spiritless,
And every move made to free the state is called virtue.
Of this you have, my lord, too certain proofs:
They have formed ten unsuccessful plots against you;
Perhaps the eleventh is ready to burst out,
And perhaps this impulse which comes to agitate you,
Is only a secret warning that heaven sends you,
As it has only this way to preserve you.
Expose yourself no more to these famous catastrophes:
It is glorious to die master of the world;
But the most glorious death stains our memory,
When we might have lived and increased our glory."

Cinna.

If the love of country ought to prevail here,
It is her good alone that you ought to desire;

And this liberty, which seems to her so dear,
Is only, my lord, an imaginary blessing to Rome,
More hurtful than useful, and which does not approach
That which a good prince brings to his states:
With order and reason he dispenses honors,
Punishes and rewards with discernment,
And disposes of all as a just owner,
Without precipitating aught for fear of a successor.
But when the people are masters they act only in tumult;
The voice of reason is never consulted;
Honors are sold to the most ambitious,
Authority given over to the most factious.
These little sovereigns whom the people make for a year,
Seeing their power limited by so short a time,
Render the fruit of the happiest designs abortive,
For fear of leaving it to him who follows them;
As they have little part in the benefits they ordain,
They gather an abundant harvest in the field of the
        public,
Assured that each one readily pardons them,
Hoping in his turn a similar treatment.
The worst of states is the democratic state.

Auguste.

And yet the only one that can please in Rome.
This hatred of kings which for five hundred years
All her children have sucked with their first milk,
Is too deeply rooted to tear it from their hearts.

17*

Maxime.

Yes, my lord, Rome is too obstinate in her disease;
Her people, who are pleased by it, flee its cure:
Their custom conquers, and not reason;
And this old error which Cinna wishes to strike down,
Is a happy error which they idolize,
By which the entire world, enslaved under their laws,
Has seen them march a hundred times upon the head of kings,
And their treasury become swollen from the plunder of their
        provinces.
What more could the best princes give them?
I dare say, my lord, that all kinds of governments are not well
        received
By all climates.   Each nation has its own, suited to its nature,
Which one could not change without doing it an injury:
Such is the law of heaven whose wise equity
Sows this diversity in the world.
The Macedonians love monarchy,
And the rest of the Greeks public liberty:
The Parthians and the Persians wish sovereigns,
And the consulate alone is good for the Romans.

Cinna.

It is true that the infinite prudence of heaven
Dispenses to each nation a different genius;
But it is not less true that this order of heaven
Changes according to times as well as according to places.
Rome has received from the kings her walls and her birth;

She holds her glory and her power from the consuls,
And receives now from your rare goodness
The sovereign complement of her prosperity.
Under you the state is no longer pillaged by armies;
The gates of Janus are closed by your hands,
Which was only seen once under her consuls,
And which the second of her kings like them brought to pass.

Maxime.

The changes of government which the divine dispensation
    makes,
Cost no blood, have in them nothing that is baleful.

Cinna.

It is a rule of the gods which never is broken,
To sell us a little dear the great blessings which they bestow
        on us.
The exile of the Tarquins even stained our lands with blood,
And our first consuls cost us some wars.

Maxime.

Then your grandfather Pompey resisted heaven
When he fought for our liberty?

Cinna.

If heaven had not wished Rome to lose it,
It would have defended it by the hands of Pompey:
It chose his death to serve worthily

As an eternal mark for this great change,
And owed to the shade of such a man this glory,
To carry away with it the liberty of Rome.
This name for a long time has only served to dazzle her,
And her own greatness hinders her from enjoying it.
Ever since she beheld herself mistress of the world,
Ever since wealth has abounded within her walls,
And her bosom, fruitful in glorious exploits,
Has produced citizens more powerful than kings ;
The great, buying suffrages to strengthen themselves,
In their pay pompously hold their masters,
Who, allowing themselves to be chained by gilded fetters,
Receive from them the laws which they think they impose upon
       them.
Thus Sulla became jealous of Marius ;
Cæsar of my grandfather ; Marc Antony of you ;
Thus liberty can no longer be useful
Save to instigate the furies of a civil war,
When in a quarrel fatal to the world,
One wishes no master, and the other no equal.
My lord, to save Rome, it is necessary that she be united
In the hand of a good chief whom all obey.
If you still love to favor her,
Take from her the means of becoming more divided.
Sulla, abandoning at last the place well usurped,
Has only opened the field to Cæsar and Pompey,
Whom the misfortune of the times would not have caused us
       to see,
If he had assured his power in his family.

What has the cruel assassination of the great Cæsar done,
But to raise against you Antony with Lepidus,
Who would not by the Romans have destroyed Rome,
If Cæsar had left the sovereignty in your hands?
By abandoning this sovereignty, you will plunge her back
Into the woes from which she yet scarcely rests;
And a new war, my lord, will exhaust her
Of the little blood which remains to her.
Let love of country, let pity touch you;
Your Rome on her knees speaks to you by my mouth.
Consider the price that you have cost:
Not that she thinks she has bought you too dear;
For the ills that she has suffered she is too well paid ;
But a just fear holds her soul affrighted ;
If, jealous of her good fortune, and weary of ruling,
You give her back a boon that she can not preserve ;
If she must at this price buy another sovereign,
If you do not prefer her interests to your own,
If this baleful gift puts her in despair,
I dare not say here what I dare foresee.
Preserve yourself, my lord, in leaving her a master
Under whom her true weal begins to revive ;
And in order to better assure the common good of all,
Give her a successor who shall be worthy of you.

At the conclusion of this speech, Auguste declares
that pity for the sad plight in which his country
would be left were he to abdicate, constrains him

in spite of his strong desire for repose to accept the
advice of Cinna and retain the sovereign power.
The Emperor then announces his intention of making Cinna his partner in the cares of state, bestows
upon him the hand of Émilie, and appoints Maxime
governor of Sicily.

This superb scene, though parts of the discussion
are pitched in a key that grates upon our American
ears, is entirely worthy of the intensely dramatic
situation, and has always been regarded by French
critics as a marvellous triumph of genius, equally
admirable for majestic language and political
wisdom. Statesmen have perceived with surprise
that Corneille was familiar with some of the profoundest secrets of their guild. Principles at which
political philosophers arrive only after long and
laborious processes of reasoning, he seems to
apprehend by the simple exercise of his poetic
intuition.

Corneille's greatness of soul at once puts him in
touch with all that is great in every walk and work
of life. The law of the correlation of forces, as we
have intimated before, is as true of the mental and
the moral as it is of the physical world. The energy

which created "Cinna" could, with the necessary environment, have created and carried out a great governmental policy.

It is exceedingly interesting to note the impression produced by this play upon the warrior statesman, Napoleon Bonaparte.

"Quel chef d'oeuvre que Cinna!" he exclaims, "comme cela est construit! comme il est évident qu' Octave, malgré les taches de sang du triumvirat, est nécessaire à l'empire, et l'empire à Rome! La première fois que j'entendis ce langage, je fus comme illuminé, et j'aperçus clairement dans la politique et dans la poésie des horizons que je n'avais pas encore soupçonnés, mais que je reconnus faits pour moi." What is this but the joyous cry of genius recognizing genius?

The next scene consists of a conversation between the two conspirators. Maxime demands to know what course Cinna is now going to pursue after his flattering words to the Emperor. Cinna replies that his purpose is unchanged. He wants Rome to be free. But he is unwilling to let the tyrant escape punishment for his crimes by putting off the purple and laying down the sceptre.

No, he must die—die in all the pomp of his power—die as a sacrifice on liberty's altar—die as a criminal whose hands are red with blood—die as a warning to all would-be usurpers in future.

Maxime takes a different view. He thinks that it would have been wiser to accept liberty when it was freely offered than to jeopardize it by a resort to violence in order to take vengeance on the tyrant. Each maintains his opinion with considerable earnestness.

Finally, Cinna suggests that, as it is very dangerous to talk about such a subject in the palace, they had better postpone their conversation until they reach a safer place. Maxime agrees, they go out, and the act closes.

A calcium light is now thrown into the dark chambers of each conspirator's heart, revealing its secret workings, its turbulent emotions.

The third act opens with a conversation between Maxime and his freedman, Euphorbe. Maxime has learned from Cinna's own mouth that his love for Émilie and his hope of winning her hand by avenging her father's death are the real reasons why he, the Emperor's trusted counsellor, has conspired against his benefactor's life and put back the cup of liberty which Auguste was holding to the lips of Rome.

This intelligence has produced in the mind of Maxime the bitterest chagrin, for, as he confesses to Euphorbe, he is passionately in love with Émilie himself, and he sees now that if this conspiracy, by which he thought to prove himself worthy of her hand, should succeed, its effect would be to crown his rival's brow with laurels and give him Émilie for his bride.   To prevent such a consummation, Euphorbe strongly urges his master to betray Cinna to Auguste. Maxime, though his better nature revolts at the base proposal, nevertheless considers its expediency with Euphorbe.

While they are discussing the matter, Cinna comes up, Euphorbe retires, and the two conspirators enter into conversation. Cinna tells how remorse, with her scorpion brood, has made her nest within his heart, how he is horrified at the thought of his black ingratitude toward the Emperor who had lavished so many favors upon him, and how against all his scruples his love for Émilie asserts its sovereign power.

18

Maxime, who has no patience with these sentiments, reproaches him sharply for advising Auguste
as he had, and calls upon him now at least to hear
the voice of Rome and join in forcibly freeing her
from the tyrant's thrall.   Cinna begs his comrade to
cease his harsh words, assures him that he will soon
repair his fault toward Rome, and finally entreats
him to leave him alone with his melancholy thoughts.
Maxime, aiming a Parthian arrow at his chagrined
accomplice in conspiracy, then withdraws.

The ensuing soliloquy of Cinna is full of passion.
As he remembers the countless favors that Auguste
has showered upon him, his soul revolts at the
thought of the dastardly deed he is pledged to do ;
his cheeks are seared by the burning blush of guilty
shame ; his base ingratitude stands revealed to him
in all its hideousness, a " marble-hearted fiend ; "
his better nature breaks forth in expostulation
against his treacherous course.   But now across the
swelling billows of passion by which his soul is
tossed he hears the ravishing strain of the Siren
Love ; he yields to her enchantment ; he throttles
protesting honor ; and the doomed bark drifts on
toward the dread reefs of disgrace.

At the conclusion of this monologue, Émilie, accompanied by her confidant, Fulvie, reappears upon the stage. During the interview between the lovers which follows, Cinna tries to persuade Émilie to forgive Auguste for the wrong he had done her in the long ago—a wrong for which he had surely made all the atonement that lay in his power. But Émilie indignantly spurns the proposal, rebukes and reproaches her lover in words of withering scorn, and finally declares her intention to slay the Emperor herself and perish with him.

This maddens Cinna. He will satisfy her, he cries; he will avenge her father; he will assassinate Auguste; and then he will recover his lost honor by burying his dagger in his own unhappy heart. With such wild words, he rushes out. Émilie is not unmoved at this outburst, as we see from the rapid colloquy which immediately ensues between her and her confidant.

Fulvie.

You have plunged his soul in despair!

Émilie.

Let him cease to love me, or let him follow his duty.

Fulvie.

He is going to obey you at the expense of his life:
You are weeping!

Émilie.

Alas! run after him, Fulvie,
And, if thy friendship deigns to aid me,
Snatch from his heart the determination to die;
Tell him . . . .

Fulvie.

That for his sake you let Auguste live?

Émilie.

Ah! that is to subject my hate to too unjust a law.

Fulvie.

And what then?

Émilie.

Let him finish his task, and redeem his faith,
And let him afterwards choose between death and me.

Once more her womanliness, like the silver moon
from under leaden clouds, shines through the dark
passions that overcast her soul. She can not entirely
annihilate her sensibilities. When love with magic
rod smites her rocky heart, tears of tenderness will
gush forth, despite her grim resolution. We are

glad it is thus; we are pleased to find that this
strange creature, so ruthless, so relentless, so ran-
corous, whom no subsequent kindness, however
loving and lavish it may be, can ever make forget
her wrong, nor forgive its author, nor forego her
vengeance, is human after all.

True, she almost at once conquers her emotion,
but it is by a great effort, and now that we have
seen this exhibition of feeling we shall be far less
offended at her stoicism, for we shall know the
terrible tension under which she is acting, and shall
realize that only a stern sense of duty to her father
drives her to pursue so desperate a course. The
above scene which concludes the third act, is one
of those brilliant strokes that bespeak the master.
Hard, indeed, would it be to conceive a more splendid conclusion.

In the first scene of act fourth, Euphorbe reveals
the plot to Auguste, telling him that Maxime now
bitterly repents his part in it, but that Cinna still
persists in his treason, and is doing his best to banish
the remorse and dissipate the fears of the other conspirators. Auguste, horror-stricken at the well-nigh
incredible news, whispers to his freedman, Polyclète,

18*

some secret instructions regarding Cinna, and orders that Maxime be told to repair to the palace that he may receive pardon from his outraged sovereign. Euphorbe thereupon lyingly declares that his master was so overcome by the consciousness of his guilt that he threw himself into the Tiber whose swift and swollen waters in the darkness soon bore him out of sight. Auguste replies that Maxime has yielded too much to remorse.

"There is no crime against me," says the Emperor, "which repentance does not efface."

Then, dismissing Euphorbe and the attendants, he gives vent to his emotions in a long monologue, now calling upon heaven to take back the fatal power whose possession has thus raised up against him his friends with poniards in their hands; now humbly confessing that, in view of his own bloody excesses, he has no right to complain of the murderous plot against himself; now working himself up into a passion against the faithless Cinna and crying out for vengeance; then sickening at the thought of more blood and punishments, despairing of crushing out treason by violence, and bidding himself rather

seek refuge in death from the ills that encompass
him ; then once more growing fierce against Cinna ;
exclaiming in a vehement address to himself :

"but at least with glory leave life,
Extinguish its torch in the blood of the ingrate ; "

and savagely gloating for a moment over the thought
of inflicting this retribution on the traitor ; then, at
the last, vibrating in painful suspense between the
impulse to die and the desire to conquer the hatred
of Rome, and reign in triumph over all his foes.

At the conclusion of this soliloquy there ensues
a scene between Auguste and Livie, in which the
Empress advises her husband, as he has in vain
tried severity hitherto, to try mercy now in Cinna's
case. Auguste, however, declares that he is going
to abdicate like Sulla. Livie earnestly opposes this
course, saying that it would be interpreted as the
effect of despair rather than of nobility of soul.
Auguste persists in his opinion and she in hers.
Finally the Emperor goes out in some irritation.

The scene now changes to the apartment of
Émilie. From Fulvie she has just heard that
Auguste has commanded Cinna to appear before

him. Yet, affected apparently by some psychical reaction, her only emotion is one of strange joy instead of one of terror. Astonished at her own entire composure, she asks whether she has correctly understood Fulvie's words. The confidant, in reply, repeats all that she knows of the matter. She says that she, having succeeded in dissuading Cinna from suicide, was bringing him back to Émilie's presence to try once more to appease her inveterate hatred, when all at once he was accosted by Polyclète who, acting by the Emperor's order, immediately conducted him to the palace.

Auguste himself is greatly perturbed about something. Évandre and Euphorbe have both been arrested and Maxime is reported to have thrown himself into the Tiber. In spite of this alarming story of Fulvie's, Émilie still remains indifferent to the imminent peril to which all the conspirators are exposed, and still feels an unaccountable exaltation of soul, an emotion which she takes to be the gift of the gods to enable her to meet death with a courage becoming the daughter of an heroic house. A moment later she is amazed to see Maxime advancing toward her.

"They told me you were dead," she cries.

Maxime.

Euphorbe deceives Auguste with that false report;
Seeing himself arrested, and the plot discovered,
He invented this death to prevent my destruction.

Émilie.

What do they say of Cinna?

Maxime.

That his greatest regret
Is to see that Cæsar knows all your secret;
In vain he denies it and wishes to feign ignorance of it;
Évandre has told all to excuse his master,
And by the order of Auguste an officer is coming to arrest you.

Émilie.

The one who received it delays to execute it;
I am ready to follow him and weary of waiting for him.

Maxime.

He awaits you at my house.

Émilie.

At your house!

Maxime.

'Tis to take you by surprise:
But learn the care that heaven has for you:
He is one of the conspirators who is going to flee with us.
Let us seize our advantage before they pursue us;
We have a boat on the river bank ready to start.

Émilie.

Dost thou know me, Maxime, and knowest thou who I am?

Thus, with fine dignity, she repulses his first advance. But he does not desist at one rebuff. Again and again he tries to overcome her cold disdain. The miserable villain makes himself positively ridiculous by the far-fetched conceits which he employs in pressing his suit. All his efforts, however, are utterly futile. Émilie with her sharp scorn pricks the brilliant bubble he had blown. She does not hesitate to tell him that she suspects him of perfidy. The essential nobility of her character shines out all through the scene in marked contrast with his despicable meanness. At length, cutting short his importunities, and declaring that she will hear him no more until they meet in the presence of the Emperor, she retires with her confidant.

Maxime, in a soliloquy, confesses that he deserves the contemptuous rejection which he has met with, expresses his belief that Émilie will at her execution tell the whole story of his infamy, speaks with chagrin of the ignominious failure of his damnable designs, bitterly accuses Euphorbe of being the author of his trouble, and in conclusion indicates his determination first to slay the freedman and then to kill himself as a sacrifice to Cinna and Émilie.

This monologue closes the fourth act which, it must be admitted, is as a whole, noticeably deficient in dramatic incident. But the critic's pen, lifted to blame this blemish, falls powerless before the grandeur of the last act.

The first scene is exceedingly brilliant. Cinna is alone with the Emperor. Auguste, after enumerating in a strain of magnificent eloquence, vivid, terse and ornate, all the signal favors which he had bestowed upon the traitor before him, charges the wretched man with his terrible crime in these cogent words:

" Thou rememberest, Cinna; so much good fortune and so much
        glory
Can not so soon escape thy memory;

But, what one could never imagine,
Cinna, thou rememberest and wishest to assassinate me."

What a powerful home thrust is that last line!

" Thou rememberest and wishest to assassinate me!"

Cinna at first attempts to deny the accusation. But Auguste, bidding him be silent, at once convicts him by giving the details of the plot and mentioning the names of the most prominent conspirators. The Emperor then excoriates the culprit with a caustic rebuke, granting him permission at its close to speak in his own defence. Cinna meets the crisis with true Roman firmness. Anxious to save Émilie, he declares that the sole cause of his treason was the desire to avenge the slaughter of his grandfather Pompey and his two sons. But not a word does the young man deign to say in excuse for his course. Not the slightest profession of penitence does he make. Not a prayer for mercy does he utter. He looks death in the face without a tremor, and calmly waits for the Emperor to wreak his vengeance. Surprised at this haughty demeanor, Auguste exclaims:

" Let us see whether thy constancy will continue even to
       the end.
Thou knowest what is thy due, thou seest I know all :
Pass sentence on thyself, and choose thy own punishments."

Just then Livie enters accompanied by Émilie
and Fulvie.

" You do not know all the accomplices," cries the Empress ;
" Your Émilie is one of them, my lord, and here she is."

Cinna.

'Tis she herself, O gods !

Auguste.

And thou, too, my daughter !

Émilie.

Yes, all that he·has done, he has done to please me,
And I, my lord, was the cause and the reward of it.

The Emperor at first thinks that the girl is simply
making a mad effort to save her lover. This idea,
however, she immediately dispels as she relates how
she fairly dragged Cinna into treason by making her
acceptance of his hand conditional upon his avenging
her father. The heart of Auguste is terribly wrung
by this new sorrow.

19

"Oh, my daughter," he cries, "is that the reward of my
    benefits?"

Émilie.

Those of my father produced in you the same effects.

Auguste.

Think with what love I reared thy youth.

Émilie.

He reared yours with the same tenderness;
He was your tutor, and you his assassin;
And you have taught me the road to crime:
Mine differs from yours in this point alone,
That your ambition sacrificed my father to itself,
And that a just wrath with which I feel myself burn,
To his innocent blood wished to sacrifice you.

At this point Livie breaks in with a protest. She
tells Émilie that Auguste has by his kindness to her
paid off only too well the debt which he owed her
father, declares that the Emperor ought not to be
held to account for the crimes of Octavius, and
maintains that, whatever be the provocation, subjects
have no right to raise their hands against the sovereign. Here Corneille unconsciously makes Livie
speak the language of the courtly casuists of the
seventeenth century. Émilie replies that she spoke

to irritate Auguste, not to defend herself. She then
bids him take her life to assure his own.

> "If I have corrupted Cinna," she exclaims, "I will seduce many
> others,
> And I am the more to be feared and you the more in danger,
> If I have love and blood both to avenge."

No sooner have these last lines fallen from her
lips than Cinna, filled with a passionate desire to
save his lover, earnestly denies that the plot originated with her. He declares that he had formed
the design before he fell in love with her, and
that, finding his suit vain at first, he had finally
won success by appealing to her feminine love
for revenge and offering to her with his heart
the service of his arm.

> "She has only conspired," he cries, "through my craft;
> I am the sole author of the plot, she is only an accomplice."

Émilie.

> Cinna, what dost thou dare say? is that to cherish me,
> To take away honor from me when I must die?

Cinna.

> Die, but in dying stain not my glory.

Émilie.

Mine is blasted, if Cæsar wishes to believe you.

Cinna.

And mine is lost if you take to yourself
All that which follows from such noble deeds.

Émilie.

Ah, well! take thy part of it and leave me mine;
'T would be to diminish it, to diminish thine:
Glory and pleasure, shame and tortures,
All ought to be in common between two lovers.
Our two souls, my lord, are two Roman souls;
In uniting our desires, we united our hates;
The lively resentment of the slaughter of our relatives
Taught us our duties in one and the same moment;
In this noble design our hearts met;
Our lofty spirits formed it together;
Together we seek the honor of a glorious death,
You wished to unite us, do not separate us.

Auguste.

Yes, I will unite you, ungrateful and perfidious couple,
And more hostile to me than is Antony or Lepidus,
Yes, I will unite you, since you wish it:
It is, indeed, necessary to satisfy the fires with which you burn,
And let all the world, knowing what incites me,
Be astonished at the punishment as well as at the crime.

We have now reached the last scene in the play —a scene which stirs some of the noblest emotions of the soul, and whose grandeur has compelled the homage of the critics of every land. Auguste, the master of the world, proves that he is also master of himself. Within his heart rages the furious passion of anger against the ingrates who had conspired to assassinate him. But by a mighty effort he conquers this desire for vengeance, pardons his enemies, and bestows upon them far greater favors than ever before.

Some dramatists, by depicting such things as the horrors of battle, the awful glare of a conflagration or the wild fury of a tempest, have attained what Coleridge called "the material sublime;" it is the glory of Corneille that not here only but time and again elsewhere, he has created matchless examples of the moral sublime. The triumph of a godlike soul over the Python passion—what could be grander than this? But let us at once turn to the inspiring spectacle. I quote the entire scene.

Auguste.

But in short heaven loves me, and its renewed favors
Have rescued Maxime from the fury of the waters.
Approach, sole friend that I find faithful.

19*

Maxime.

Honor less, my lord, a criminal soul.

Auguste.

Speak no more of crime after thy repentance,
After thou hast saved me from peril:
'Tis to thee that I owe both life and empire.

Maxime.

Know better the worst of all your enemies:
If you reign still, my lord, if you live,
It is to my jealous rage that you owe it.
A virtuous remorse has not touched my soul;
To destroy my rival I have disclosed his plot.
Euphorbe pretended to you that I had drowned myself,
For fear that you had sent after me:
I wished to have the means of deceiving Émilie,
Terrifying her mind, drawing her away from Italy,
And thought to reconcile her to this abduction
Under the hope of returning to avenge her lover;
But instead of tasting these gross baits,
Her virtue redoubled its energies by being attacked.
She read into my heart.   You know the rest,
And it would be superfluous for me to recite it to you.
You see the success of my base stratagem.
If, however, some thanks are due my information,
Cause Euphorbe to perish in the midst of torture,
And suffer me to die before the eyes of these lovers.

I have betrayed my friend, my lover, my master,
My glory, my country, by the advice of this traitor;
And yet I will think my good fortune infinite,
If I can punish myself for it after having punished him.

Auguste.

Is it enough, O heaven! and to injure me
Has fate any other of my intimates whom it wishes to seduce?
Let it join to its efforts the help of Hades;
I am master of myself as well as of the world:
I am, I will to be. O centuries! O memory!
Preserve forever my last victory;
I triumph to-day over the most righteous wrath
Whose remembrance can go down to you.
Let us be friends, Cinna, it is I who invite thee:
I have given thee life as to my enemy;
And, in spite of the fury of thy base design,
I give it to thee again as to my assassin.
Let us begin a combat that shall show by the issue
Which of us has done better, I in giving or thou in receiving it.
Thou didst betray my favors, I wish to redouble them;
I had loaded you with them, I wish to overwhelm you with
    them:
With this beautiful woman whom I had given thee
Receive the consulate for the next year.
Love Cinna, my daughter, in this illustrious station;
Prefer its purple to that of my blood;
Learn by my example to conquer thy anger:
By giving thee back a husband, I give thee back more than a
    father.

Émilie.

I yield, my lord, to these noble kindnesses;
I recover my vision by their light:
I recognize my fault which seemed to me justice;
And, what the terror of punishment could not have caused,
I feel arise in my soul a strong repentance,
And my heart in secret tells me that it consents to it.
Heaven has ordained your supreme greatness;
And for proof, my lord, I need only myself.
I dare with vanity take to myself this honor,
That since heaven changes my heart, it wishes to change the
        state.
My hate, which I thought immortal, is going to die;
It is dead, and this heart becomes a faithful subject;
And as it conceives henceforth a horror for this hate,
The ardor of serving you succeeds its fury.

Cinna.

My lord, what shall I say to you, after our offences
Instead of punishments find rewards?
O, virtue without example!   O, clemency, which renders
Your power juster, and my crime greater.

Auguste.

Cease to delay a magnanimous forgetfulness of it;
And do both of you with me render thanks to Maxime:
He has betrayed us all; but what he has done
Preserves you innocent, and gives me back my friends.

(to Maxime)

Resume thy wonted place near me;
Enter again into thy power and into thy renown;
Let Euphorbe from all three have pardon in his turn,
And to-morrow let marriage crown their love.
If thou lovest her still, that shall be thy punishment.

Maxime.

I do not murmur at it, it has too much justice;
And I am more confused, my lord, by your kindness
Than I am jealous of the boon that you take from me.

Cinna.

Suffer my virtue, called back into my heart,
To consecrate to you a faith basely violated,
But so firm now, so far from wavering
That the fall of the skies could not shake it.
May the great author of noble destinies,
Cut short our years in order to prolong your days;
And may I by a good fortune of which each one shall be jealous
Lose for you a hundred times what I receive from you.

Livie.

That is not all, my lord; a celestial flame
With a prophetic ray illumines my soul.
Hear what the gods make known to you through me;
It is the immutable law of your happy destiny.
After this action you have nothing to fear;

The state will bear the yoke henceforth without complaining;
And the most untractable, abandoning their projects,
Will find all their glory in dying your subjects;
No base design, no ungrateful envy
Will attack the course of so noble a life;
Never any more assassins nor conspirators:
You have found the art of being master of hearts.
Rome, with a joy both keen and deep,
Resigns into your hands the empire of the world;
Your kingly virtues will teach her too well
That her happiness consists in causing you to reign:
From so long an error fully freed,
She no longer has any prayers save for the monarchy,
Already is preparing for you temples and altars,
And heaven is preparing for you a place among the immortals;
And posterity in every nation
Will give your example to the noblest princes.

Auguste.

I accept the prophecy and I dare hope it:
Thus always may the gods deign to inspire you!
To-morrow let the happy sacrifices be doubled
Which we shall offer them under better auspices,
And let your fellow conspirators hear it proclaimed
That Auguste has learned all, and wishes to forget all.

So ends this great play. Its chief defect as a
drama is that it has too little action and too much

debate. This, however, does not mar the beauty of the piece as a poem. Statesmen have always admired the historic insight and the knowledge of state-craft shown by Corneille in the political discussions. Voltaire tells us that of all the great poet's tragedies Cinna was the favorite of the court. It is easy to discover the reason. The play contained the idealized expression of the dominant political beliefs of the time. Corneille's characters said in magnificent rhetoric what the spectators believed and felt. Then there was that grand closing scene.

As Auguste pronounced his immortal "Soyons amis, Cinna," the old nobility of France felt the finest chords of their hearts thrown into sympathetic vibration ; the great Condé wept manly tears; and the whole assemblage were lifted out of themselves and raised to the empyreal heights of generous sentiment.

Nor was the piece destined to lose its power to move the hearts of men. Succeeding generations have yielded their sincere tribute to the genius of our poet. Louis XV is reported as saying, after a representation of Cinna, that he was so affected by the passage to which reference was just made that, if any one had at that moment demanded from him the pardon of Cardinal Rohan, he could not have refused.   Corneille was, indeed, worthy to be called the breviary of kings.

CHAPTER VI.

The Great Dramatist at the Meridian of His Glory: Polyeucte.

THE next creation of our author's genius was *Polyeucte*. One evening in the year 1640, Corneille read the new piece before the cultured coterie who were wont to gather at the Hôtel de Rambouillet. The literary men of the period entertained the highest respect for this tribunal. Few ventured to dispute its verdict upon any question of taste. So powerful was the influence exerted upon French letters by the *Hôtel*, that we must pause long enough to say a word as to its history and function.

On the 26th of January, 1600, Charles d'Angennes, a high-born nobleman, then vidame du Mans, afterwards Marquis de Rambouillet, married Catherine de Vivonne, daughter of Jean de Vivonne, sieur de Saint-Gohard, afterwards first Marquis de Pisani,

and Julia Savelli, widow of Luis des Ursins and herself descended from the noble Italian family of the Strozzi.   Both the Marquis and the Marquise de Rambouillet were thus of illustrious lineage.

When they came to live at Paris, the refined nature of the Marquise, who was as good as she was beautiful, was shocked at the frivolity, grossness and immorality which then characterized the court.   Withdrawing from an atmosphere so unwholesome, she rebuilt the Hôtel de Rambouillet, and on its completion in 1617 opened her doors to a select circle of friends and acquaintances.

In a little while she had gathered around her a bright galaxy of virtue, beauty and wit, established a literary *Salon*, and so introduced a new element into the fashionable life of the capital.

The distinguished company who frequented the Hôtel devoted themselves enthusiastically to the great tasks of purifying the morals, polishing the manners, refining the language and elevating the literature of the time.   The Italian and the Spanish influences of which I have previously spoken met and mingled here.   Conversation was cultivated as a fine art, the proprieties of life were authoritatively promulgated, and polite society sprang into existence.

The necessity for female education was eloquently set forth, especially by Mlle. de Scudéry. With unanswerable logic she maintained that woman must be fitted for companionship with her husband, that her individuality must be developed, and that she must be permitted to stand upon the same social plane.

Thus every noble ideal found earnest champions in the company who were drawn to the Hôtel de Rambouillet, as by a potent centripetal force.

Of course the society had its failings. Overrefinement sometimes ran into affectation. Platonic attachments took the place of love. The cultivated lady became a "Blue-Stocking." The purist prepared the way for the *précieuse*.

In 1640, however, the Hôtel de Rambouillet, then in its greatest brilliancy, was the Sanhedrim of society, literature and art. Corneille, therefore, was naturally anxious to obtain the judgment of this critical audience before allowing his play to be put upon the stage. He was listened to with profound attention, and applauded as politeness required, but the real opinion of the assembly was adverse to the piece.

This became evident a few days afterward when Voiture, who had been commissioned by his associate critics to perform that disagreeable duty, delicately intimated to Corneille that Polyeucte in the judgment of the Hôtel was not altogether a success, and that his attempt to introduce religion into the drama had been especially censured.

Corneille was utterly dismayed. He knew that the verdict of the critics of the Hôtel de Rambouillet, where he was held in high esteem, was entirely sincere. He saw no resource, therefore, but to withdraw the play from the hands of the actors who were already committing it to memory. He had decided upon this course, when he was dissuaded from it by the earnest protests of one of the company of actors—a man of such inferior talents that he had not for that reason been included in the caste for the play. Posterity reversing the decision of the Hôtel de Rambouillet has endorsed the opinion of the obscure actor.

As we proceed in our study of the play, we shall find new reasons for adding our parts to that monument of praise, *aere perennius*, which each successive generation is building higher and higher to the memory of the great Corneille.

The tragedy was suggested by a passage in the historian Surius. The substance of this passage is that in Armenia, during the reign of Decius who, it will be remembered, subjected the Christians to a rigorous persecution, an Armenian named Polyeuctes having by the persuasion of his friend Nearchus become a Christian and being fired with a convert's enthusiasm, tore into shreds the edicts published against his sect, snatched the idols from the hands of those in the temple who were holding them up to be worshipped, and dashed them to pieces, for which, after his wife Paulina had vainly tried to win him from his new faith by the power of her tears, he was executed by order of his father-in-law Felix, the officer commissioned by the Emperor to enforce his cruel decrees.

Corneille took these dry bones of fact, articulated them into the skeleton of a drama, clothed them with the proper connective tissue, and breathed into the organism the breath of life.

Being thus based upon the story of a Saint, *Polyeucte* is really a miracle-play cast in the classic
20*

mould.   But there was in this noble work of genius
none of the barbarism of the mediaeval drama.
Never since " the lofty, grave tragedians " of Greece
preached their solemn sermons on divine predestina-
tion, had religious emotion been so worthily portrayed upon the stage.

The scene of the piece is laid at Melitene, the
capital of Armenia, in the palace of Félix, whom
Corneille represents as governor of the province.
The play opens with a dialogue between Polyeucte
and Néarque.   Polyeucte is fully determined to
embrace Christianity, and earnestly desires to be
baptized without another hour's delay, but Pauline
who, though she knows nothing of her husband's
design, has been visited during the preceding night
by a dream of dire portent, has tearfully besought
him not to leave the palace for any purpose whatever to-day, and he, while attaching no importance
to the dream, is loth to disregard her entreaties.
Néarque exhorts him not to postpone for so slight a
reason the performance of a solemn duty, points out
to him how liable procrastination is to lead to luke-
warmness or even cold indifference, and warns him
against allowing himself to be ensnared in this way

by the wiles of "the enemy of the human race."
Polyeucte, after defending for some minutes his
proposal for delay, yields at last to the arguments of
Néarque and cries out : " Let me flee, since I must."

Just then Pauline, accompanied by her confidant
Stratonice, comes upon the stage. Polyeucte, bidding his sweet young bride good-bye, and assuring
her that he will return in an hour at the latest,
hastens away with Néarque in spite of the springing
tears in Pauline's eyes. Left alone with Stratonice,
the troubled wife is moved by a very natural impulse
to talk about the matter which fills her heart with
foreboding. Stratonice encourages her to do so.

"In telling one's troubles," says the confidant, "one often finds
solace for them."

To better explain the ominous nature of her dream,
Pauline relates the story of the attachment which
before her marriage with Polyeucte she had cherished
for Sévère, a young Roman knight. At the mention of this name, Stratonice interrupts her to inquire
whether this is the same gallant warrior who, in a
recent battle with the Persians, after rescuing his
Emperor from the enemy and turning a Roman

defeat into a victory, had fallen on the field of his
fame among the corpses of so many foes that his
comrades had not been able to recover his body,
though his memory had been appropriately honored
by Decius.

" Alas ! 'twas he himself," cries Pauline, " and never has our
      Rome
  Produced a greater heart nor seen a more honorable man."

Continuing her story, she says that she and Sévère
both freely expressed the passion which each felt for
the other.   But, as Sévère was poor, her father forbade their marriage, and she bowed to his paternal
authority, though her obedience tore out by the
roots from her bleeding heart the fairest flower of
hope.   When Félix was made governor of Armenia,
she accompanied him to his province.   Sévère in
despair joined the army.   Thus the separation of
the two lovers was complete.

Scarcely had Félix and Pauline become acquainted
in Armenia, when a new suitor for her hand appeared.
This was Polyeucte.   Félix was delighted.   Polyeucte was the leader of the Armenian nobility.   Such
an alliance would immensely strengthen the governor

politically. He, therefore, compelled his daughter to marry the influential nobleman. Whether she loved him or not was in the sight of the sordid Félix a matter of little importance.

Thus cruelly constrained for a second time by her father, Pauline nevertheless again obeyed him meekly, and has even succeeded in developing a real affection for her husband. With these words of introduction, she then relates her dream.

"I saw him this night," says she, "this unfortunate Sévère,
Vengeance in his hand, his eye burning with anger:
He was not covered with those miserable rags
Which a sorrowful shade bears forth from the tomb;
He was not pierced by those glorious wounds
Which, cutting off his life, assure his fame;
He seemed triumphant, and like our Cæsar
When he enters Rome victorious upon his chariot.
After a little terror that the sight of him inspired in me,
'Bestow upon whom you wish the affection which is due to me,
Ingrate,' said he to me, 'and when this day has expired,
Weep at thy leisure for the husband whom thou hast preferred
          to me.'
At these words I shuddered, my soul became troubled;
Then an impious assembly of the Christians,
To hasten the accomplishment of this fatal speech,
Threw Polyeucte at the feet of his rival.

Suddenly I called my father to his help.
Alas! of the whole dream this is what plunges me into despair.
I saw my father himself, a dagger in his hand,
Enter with his arm raised to pierce his breast:
There my excessive grief mixed these images;
The blood of Polyeucte satisfied their rage.
I know not how or when they killed him,
But I know that all contributed to his death.
Behold, that is my dream."

Stratonice, while acknowledging that the vision is horrible enough in itself, seeks with sensible words to quiet Pauline's apprehensions. Can she fear a dead man? asks the confidant. Can she fear a father? Especially when he is bound to Polyeucte by so many ties of interest?

Pauline says that her father laughingly tells her the same thing. Still she is not satisfied. She is haunted by the fear that the Christians, enraged by the bloody persecutions of her father, will wreak vengeance for their wrongs upon Polyeucte. Stratonice tries to dispel this idea also. The Christians, she says, attack only the gods, and not men.

A moment later Félix enters, followed by Albin, his confidant. Félix is greatly perturbed.

My daughter," he exclaims, "into what strange terrors
Does thy dream plunge me as well as thee!
How I fear its results which seem to approach!"

Pauline.

What sudden alarm can thus dismay you?

Félix.

Sévère is not dead.

Pauline.

What harm does his life do us?

Here we see the touch of the master. "*Sévère is not dead.*" What emotions these words awaken in the heart of Pauline! Does that short sentence, like a flash of lightning, illuminate for a moment the profoundest depths of her soul, and show her that she loves Sévère still? Is she seized with a shiver of dread lest her dream be beginning to be realized? Notice the naïve response that she makes to her father's statement. "*What harm does his life do us?*" Is this love, springing forward spontaneously to champion the loved one's cause? To his daughter's last question, Félix answers that Sévère has become the favorite of the Emperor. Pauline thinks that this is no more than right.

" Destiny," she adds, " so often unpropitious to great souls,
Sometimes resolves to do them justice."

Félix.

He is coming here himself.

Pauline.

He is coming !

Félix.

Thou art going to see him.

Pauline.

That is too much ; but how can you know it ?

Félix refers to Albin as his authority, and requests
him to tell Pauline what he knows. Thereupon
Albin, passing quickly over the points already
familiar to Pauline tells how Sévère, who was
apparently dead, was carried off the field of battle
by order of the Persian king, nursed back to life
and strength, offered every inducement to espouse
the cause of Rome's enemies, and at length, after
declining all these overtures, permitted by exchange
to return to the camp of Decius.

Soon another combat occurs, continues Albin ; the
Romans are surprised ; their ranks thrown into dis-

order; disastrous rout seems inevitable. But Sévère rallies the panic-stricken troops, leads them with dauntless courage against the foe, and gains such an overwhelming victory that the Persian monarch is compelled humbly to sue for peace. This great exploit lends new lustre to the young hero's already brilliant fame. The Emperor treats him with the greatest affection. Thus it happens that, decorated with honors by his prince and idolized by the army, Sévère is now coming to bring into Armenia the glorious news of the war and to offer there a sacrifice to the gods for their timely succor.

When Albin has concluded, Félix expresses to his daughter the apprehensions which rack his mind. This sacrifice to the gods, he says, is only a pretext. The real reason of the coming of Sévère is a desire to urge again his suit for the hand of Pauline, of whose marriage he is still ignorant. When he discovers the bitter truth, will he not give rein to his resentment; will he not, by employing his great influence with Decius, work their irreparable ruin?

Pauline declares that Sévère is too noble for that, but her words utterly fail to allay her father's fears,

21

and he begs her to save him by exerting the sovereign power which she possesses over Sévère. Pauline shrinks from meeting her former lover. She is conscious that in spite of herself she still feels affection for him, she remembers that hers is a woman's heart, and she is frightened at the thought of the desperate war of emotions that would probably arise in her soul, if she should consent to see Sévère. She is not fearful lest she may fail in wifely duty; not at all; she is simply prudent; she does not wish to walk with open eyes into temptation.

Félix, however, will not listen to reason, so Pauline reluctantly promises to comply with his request, and the first act comes to a close.

The opening scene of the second act is a conversation between Sévère and Fabian, his servant. Sévère is impatient to see Pauline. He acknowledges that love of her, and not the desire to offer sacrifice, has brought him to Armenia. Through Fabian he has already sent her a message requesting her to grant him an interview. He is anxious now to learn her reply to this message. Fabian has, of course, been told by Pauline of her marriage. He wishes, however, to break the terrible news as gently as possible to his master. Hence when Sévère eagerly asks whether he will be able to see her, Fabian merely answers,

"You shall see her, my lord."

Sévère, in his joy, suspects nothing from the gravity of his servant's tone nor from the brevity of his reply. The ardent lover thinks only of his prospects of success.

Does Pauline still love him? he asks. Does mention of his coming bring the conscious blushes to her cheek? Dare he hope a blissful future from this interview?

"You shall see her," says Fabian again, "that is all I can tell you."

Then it is that Sévère begins to suspect that all is not well.

"Does she no longer love me?" he cries, "clear up this point for me."

Avoiding a direct reply, Fabian urges his master to conquer his passion for Pauline, and seek among the grand ladies of Rome a companion better suited

to his own exalted position. But the loyal heart of
Sévère scorns a proposition so base. Wealth, rank,
glory—these all he prizes only as bright flowers
which he may weave into a bridal wreath for the
lady of his love. Again Fabian urges him to give
Pauline up, and again Sévère repels the proposal,
and demands to be told whether her heart has grown
cold toward him. Fabian can now no longer conceal the terrible truth.

Fabian.

I tremble to tell you; she is . . . .

Sévère.

What?

Fabian.

Married.

Sévère is stunned by the cruel blow. " Married!
Married! " The word is the death knell of his
hopes. The bright morning of his life is overcast
by storm-clouds of misfortune. Before him, like a
wintry waste in drear Siberia, stretches the bleak
and dismal future. " Weary, stale, flat and un-
profitable " seem to him " all the uses of this

world." He prays the gods to let him die. But, even when his heart is thus swept as by a tornado of passion, he still is able to be just. On being told whom Pauline has wedded, he acknowledges that she has made a good choice, and when Fabian advises him not to see her lest he should forget himself and give vent to some unseemly reproach, he replies that he has no reproaches to make, that she has but done her duty, that her father in vetoing his suit only showed a proper concern for her welfare, and that his own ill-fortune has been the cause of all his misery.

Fairness like this under circumstances so trying is the mark of a truly noble character. Relieved to see his master in such an equitable frame of mind, Fabian says that he will take the reassuring news to Pauline, who like himself had feared that on meeting her Sévère would be betrayed by his emotions into some distressing outbreak.

But at that moment Pauline herself appears, Stratonice, as usual, accompanying her.

"Fabian, I see her," exclaims Sévère.

Fabian.

My lord, remember . . . .

21*

Sévère.

Alas! she loves another! another is her husband!

The conversation which follows between the two former lovers is full of pathetic interest. There could hardly be a more delicate situation. These two people love; they must not love; they can not help but love.

Corneille has admirably managed the meeting. Pauline is perfectly frank. She informs Sévère in the beginning that the report of his death had not influenced her to marry. Then she tells him how deep an affection she had cherished for him. If the gods, she says, had given her the right to choose for herself, she would have preferred him to the greatest of monarchs. But her father bade her wed another, and she obeyed, for a father's will is always a Roman maiden's duty. She would have done the same thing whoever had been the husband selected for her—yes, even though she had hated him. In that case she would by an exercise of her sovereign reason have suppressed her love for Sévère and have eradicated from her heart all dislike for her husband.

These words, as one may imagine, grate harshly upon the ear of Sévère. We can readily pardon the sarcastic tone of his reply. Pauline's course seems very strange to him. He can not understand how a passion like love can be thus reduced into absolute subjection to reason. His words have in them, therefore, a sharp metallic ring of reproach. He feels, and he expresses, something very like contempt for an affection so tractable as Pauline's.

"O too lovable object," he exclaims, in conclusion, "O too
    lovable object, who too much have charmed me!
Is that how one loves, and have you loved me?"

Pauline's answer is admirable. With touching candor, she tells him just what her feelings toward him are. She has loved him, she loves him still, and this very hour the battle is raging fiercely in her heart between her passionate affection for him and her dutiful affection for Polyeucte. There is, indeed, no doubt as to which will be victorious. Her virtue is more than equal to every assault of passion. But her heart is, nevertheless, torn and harrowed and scarred by contending emotions.

This frank avowal at once disarms the chivalric Sévère. He begs Pauline to pardon the "blind grief" which made him stigmatize as inconstancy what he now sees was really a noble obedience to duty.

After the two have thus reached an understanding of each other's feelings, Pauline entreats Sévère, as he values her spotless reputation and peace of mind, to seek no more interviews with her. Such meetings, she says, only cause them both acuter pain.

Hard, indeed, does it seem to Sévère to be thus shut out forever from the presence of her whom he has so fondly loved, but Pauline is firm, and he is compelled to bid her a sad good-bye, telling her that he is going to seek a warrior's death as the only solace for his bitter sorrow.

The last few lines in the scene, spoken while Sévère and Pauline still linger for a moment longer in each other's company, are strikingly beautiful. Pauline has just told Sévère that while he is at the sacrifice she is going to pray secretly to the gods in his behalf.

" May just heaven," he responds, "content with my ruin,
Crown with good fortune and length of days Polyeucte and
Pauline."

Pauline.

After so much misfortune may Sévère find
A happiness worthy of his valor !

Sévère.

He found it in you.

Pauline.

I was dependent upon a father.

Sévère.

O duty which ruins me and which plunges me in despair !
Farewell, too virtuous object, and too charming.

Pauline.

Farewell, too unfortunate and too perfect lover.

What a pity that the last two execrable lines
should have been added to mar the beauty of the
others. Here, again, we see the shadow of the
affected gallantry of the times falling even upon
the bright page of Corneille.

Sévère and Fabian now withdraw and Pauline is
left alone with Stratonice. The confidant, who feels
a sincere compassion for the woebegone young wife
tries to console her with the reflection that at least
her dream has been proved false, since, though Sévère

has indeed appeared, he evidently cherishes no thought
of vengeance.   But Pauline is not thus to be comforted.   The awful picture of the horrors which she
saw in her dream is continually rising up before her
mind.   It is in vain that she remembers the generous words of Sévère.   Bleeding Polyeucte is ever
appearing to her view.   She can not but feel anxious
as long as Sévère remains in the vicinity.

"To whatever his virtue may dispose him," she exclaims,
"He is powerful, he loves me, and comes to marry me."

At this moment Polyeucte and Néarque enter.
Polyeucte, finding Pauline in tears, and erroneously
supposing that they are caused by the apprehensions
to which her dream has given rise, bids her dry her
eyes and dismiss her fears, for despite the ominous
vision, he has returned to her safe and sound.
Pauline reminds him that the day is yet far from
being over, and declares that her dream has already
come true in part, since Sévère, whom she believed
dead, has suddenly made his appearance in their city.

Polyeucte replies that he is aware of this, but it
causes him no concern.   He is in Melitene; Félix
is governor of the province; and Polyeucte himself

is a leading citizen.   Why should he feel at all dismayed?   Moreover, Sévère would never stoop to take such a base revenge.   His soul is too noble for that. Polyeucte adds that he came to pay his respects to Sévère who, he had been told, was making a visit to Pauline.

" He has just left me very sad and troubled," Pauline answers, "But I have persuaded him to see me no more."

Polyeucte.

What! you suspect me already of some distrust?

Pauline.

I should offer to all three too grievous an affront.

After making this admirable response, Pauline gives the reason which did move her to banish Sévère from her sight.   We have already heard her express similar ideas.   She is entirely confident of her power to withstand all temptation ; she fears no stain upon the immaculate robe of virtue in which she is clad; but she wisely wishes to avoid the throes of combat.

Polyeucte is expressing his admiration for his wife's beautiful character, when he receives from

Félix through Cléon, the servant of the governor, a summons to repair at once to the temple, as the sacrifice is now ready to begin. Without delay Polyeucte and Néarque set out for the scene of the ceremony, while Pauline remains in the palace.

Astonished at first that Polyeucte should go near a temple where pagan worship was being offered, Néarque expresses his own abhorrence of false gods, and earnestly advises his friend to flee from their altars.

Then Polyeucte reveals his purpose in going to the sacrifice. He is determined to brave paganism in its citadel; he will assail the false gods in the temple itself; he will break their images before the very eyes of the worshippers; he will deal idolatry once for all a crushing blow. Such fierce enthusiasm staggers even the fervid Néarque himself.

"This zeal," he remonstrates, "is too ardent, suffer it to moderate."

Polyeucte.

One can not have too much for the God whom one reveres.

Néarque.

You will meet death.

Polyeucte.

I seek it for Him.

Néarque.

And if this courage fail?

Polyeucte.

He will be my support.

Néarque.

He does not command that one should rush precipitately to death.

Polyeucte.

The more voluntary it is, the more it merits.

Néarque.

It is sufficient, without seeking it, to await and to suffer it.

Polyeucte.

One suffers with regret when one dares not offer himself.

Néarque.

But in short, death is certain in this temple.

Polyeucte.

But in the skies already the palm is prepared.

22

Néarque.

It is necessary to merit it by a holy life.

Polyeucte.

My crimes during life might take it away from me.
Why subject to chance what death assures?
When it opens heaven, can it seem hard?
I am a Christian, Néarque, and am one to the core;
The faith that I have aspires to its consummation.
He who flees believes as a coward, and has only a dead faith.

Néarque.

Take care of your life; it is important to God himself;
Live to protect the Christians in these places.

Polyeucte.

The example of my death will fortify them better.

Néarque.

You wish then to die?

Polyeucte.

You love then to live?

Néarque.

I can not disguise the fact that it is hard for me to follow you.
I fear lest I may succumb under the horror of the tortures.

Polyeucte.

He who walks surely has no fear of falling:
God bestows in time of need His infinite strength.
He who fears lest he may deny Him, in his soul does deny Him;
He believes that He is able to succor, and doubts His faithfulness.

Néarque.

He who fears nothing presumes too much upon himself.

Polyeucte.

I look for everything from His grace and nothing from my
   weakness.
But far from urging me, it is necessary that I urge you!
Whence comes this coldness?

Néarque.

   God himself feared death.

Polyeucte.

He offered himself, nevertheless; let us imitate this holy effort;
Let us raise altars to Him upon heaps of idols.
It is necessary, I remember still your words,
To neglect, in order to please Him, wife and goods and rank;
To expose and shed for His glory all one's blood.
Alas! what have you done with that perfect love
Which you wished for me, and which I wish for you?
If some of it remains in you still, are you not jealous

That, though I have just become a Christian, I show more of
  it than you?

Emotion is contagious. The flaming zeal of
Polyeucte leaps forth from his heart, enwraps the
soul of Néarque, and in a moment both are glowing
with the most intense religious fervor. The modera-
tion of Néarque has melted entirely away before this
fiery enthusiasm. Forgotten now are all his fears
of death. He feels within him a hero's eagerness
to do and die. Completely possessed by such passionate ardor, the two friends hasten on to the
temple. Thus we reach the end of the second act.

We must now return to Pauline. She is not yet
able to banish from her mind the feeling of apprehension inspired by her dreadful dream. In the
first scene of act third she expresses her fears in a
long soliloquy which is rather cold because it contains too much reasoning and too little passion.
Pauline is afraid now that when Polyeucte and
Sévère meet at the temple a fatal quarrel may, in
spite of their chivalrous attitude toward each other,
be precipitated between them. It needs but a word,
she reasons, to put rivals at daggers' points. Should

such a quarrel occur, what could save Polyeucte from destruction? Owing to his powerful influence with Decius, Sévère could crush his adversary like a moth. Félix would never dare to interfere. He might not even wish to do so. Such are the fears that torment the mind of Pauline. As she concludes her soliloquy, Stratonice enters.

Pauline eagerly asks for news of the sacrifice. Alas! her dark forebodings are now to be fully justified. With vehement indignation Stratonice tells her how Polyeucte has become a Christian; how he and Néarque have just outraged the religious sentiment of the city; how they have insulted the deities in the temple, proclaiming that there is but one God, the God of the Christians, dashing to the floor the holy sacrificial vases, and throwing down the statue of Jupiter himself; how these fanatical acts, committed in defiance of the authority of Félix, have set the congregation in an uproar; and how, fearing the wrath of the gods, the people have finally fled from the temple with loud cries of horror and rage.

Pauline, of course, is greatly shocked at hearing this recital. But in spite of her husband's sacrilegious conduct, as she regards it, she decides that

22*

duty requires her still to cleave to him with wifely affection. Truer heart than hers never beat in the breast of woman.

After relating the above facts in graphic style, Stratonice is about to tell what action Félix has taken, when the governor himself appears upon the scene. He is very angry. Néarque, he declares, shall die. As for Polyeucte, Félix says that he still feels a fatherly affection for him in spite of his atrocious behavior. He will, therefore, be given opportunity to recant his profession of the hated faith. Félix hopes that the execution of Néarque, which Polyeucte will be compelled to witness, will so shatter this young enthusiast's nerves that he will be glad to yield in order to save himself from a similar fate.

Pauline knows her husband better. She is certain that he will stand as firm as a Doric pillar for what he believes is right. Death, she is well aware, has no terrors for the Christian. Polyeucte will meet martyrdom with joyous fortitude. She, therefore, beseeches her father not to make the forgiveness of her husband conditional upon his recantation, since this is a condition which can never be fulfilled—but to pardon him absolutely. All her pleading, however, is in vain. Félix is obdurate. If Polyeucte persists in his course, his blood be on his head.

Pauline is still engaged in her fruitless attempt to move her father to mercy, when Albin enters with important news. Néarque, he says, has been put to death. But the execution has been very far from having the desired effect upon Polyeucte. Instead of being terrified by the awful spectacle, he seems to be burning with the desire to follow his friend to death. This is precisely what Pauline expected. Again she implores her father to revoke his stern decree, urging upon him that Polyeucte is the husband whom he himself chose for her, reminding him that at his command she had smothered her love for Sévère, and modestly pleading her whole life of filial obedience. But it is all of no avail. Félix still denies her prayer, becomes irritated at her persistency, and at last requests her to leave him alone with Albin.

The conversation which ensues between the two men after Pauline and her confidant have withdrawn reveals how large is the quantity and how base is the quality of the alloy in the character of

Félix. His mind is sorely vexed. Affection for Polyeucte, a desire to save his life, anger at seeing him develop into a fanatical Christian, dread of the wrath of the gods if his gross insult to their divinity be not avenged, fear of the displeasure of Decius if his strict orders to punish the hated sect be not carried out, all these emotions are ebbing and flowing in the heart of the perplexed governor. Albin advises him to write to the Emperor and request him to pardon Polyeucte.

The reply of Félix, though in character, is greatly lacking in plausibility. He says that he fears that, if he should do this, Sévère enraged at the escape of Polyeucte, the rival who had won over him the woman of his love, would use his tremendous influence with Decius to work the ruin of Félix himself by way of revenge. Perhaps, continues the governor, Sévère intends when Polyeucte shall have been executed to sue again for the hand of Pauline. If this be true, how terribly angry the young warrior would be, should Félix thwart him a second time in his hopes by saving his rival.

The next moment the governor shocks us by an exhibition of moral turpitude. From the deepest and darkest abysm of his soul comes the infamous thought that he would be greatly advanced in his political career, if Polyeucte should be put to death and Sévère should wed Pauline. This Satanic suggestion, he confesses, awakes in his heart "a malign joy." He condemns such thoughts as base, however, and expresses the wish that heaven's lightning may smite him rather than that he should yield to them.

"Your heart is too good," says the honest Albin, "and your soul too lofty."

Too good and too lofty, he means, to succumb to such a temptation.

In reply to a question by the confidant, Félix declares that he is unable to decide as yet what he will do if his son-in-law continues obstinate. Albin then says that the people of the city are rising up in revolt to protest against the punishment of Polyeucte, and that there is danger lest the prison may be forced. Félix answers that it will be necessary then to bring the prisoner to the palace. Accordingly they go out forthwith to take this precaution. Thus the act ends.

We are now nearing those sublime passages which
entitle *Polyeucte* to a place forever among the most
glorious productions of the literary genius of man.
All that we have as yet examined is but the golden
setting for the clustered jewels whose dazzling sheen
is soon to enchant our eyes.

As the curtain rises on the first scene of act fourth,
we behold Polyeucte confined in the palace under
the surveillance of Cléon and three other guards.
Cléon informs the prisoner that Pauline desires to
see him.   Polyeucte realizes full well how severe a
trial it will be for him to meet his wife.

"O presence!" he cries, "O combat that I dread above all!"

He begins immediately, however, to prepare for
this new ordeal.   Uttering a quick prayer for divine
succor, and calling also upon the departed spirit
of his beloved Néarque to aid him, he dispatches
Cléon with a message to Sévère, requesting him to
come at once to see the doomed Polyeucte as he
wishes before dying to tell him an important secret.

The other guards then turn aside and stand aloof,
while Polyeucte nerves his soul for the meeting with
Pauline by singing a song in which he renounces

the vanities of earth, prophesies the downfall of Decius, bids defiance to the fury of Félix, extols the joys of the Christian faith, and expresses a firm confidence of victory over the seductions of human affection in the painful interview now about to take place.

Here we reach one of those famous passages of which we spoke a moment since. Pauline enters. She has come to try upon the resolute Polyeucte all the power of her tender persuasion. A Venus in beauty, she stands *lacrimis oculos suffusa nitentes*, and pleads her cause with pathetic eloquence.

What a scene is this! Love of Pauline and love of God rend the heart of Polyeucte in their desperate combat. The power of earth is pitted against the power of heaven. The battle must needs be sublime. Such themes are admirably suited to the genius of our author.

Corneille is the Thor of the French Asgard. The tempestuous sublime is his element. Girding his belt of strength about him, putting on his iron gauntlets and grasping his mighty hammer, he knits his brows into storm-clouds, and flashes forth lightnings from his eyes and wakes the sleeping thunders as he drives his loud rumbling chariot over the loftiest peaks of human passion. Here we have him at his best. The scene is so supremely grand that we give it entire.

Polyeucte.

Madam, what design makes you ask for me?
Is it to oppose me, or to aid me?
Does this noble effort of your perfect love
Come to help me or does it come to defeat me?
Do you bring hither hatred or friendship,
As my enemy, or the loved half of my heart?

Pauline.

You have here no enemy but yourself;
You alone hate yourself when everybody loves you;
You alone bring to pass all that I have dreamed:
Will not to destroy yourself, and you are saved.
To whatever extremity your crime may go,
You are innocent if you pardon yourself.
Deign to consider the blood from which you are descended,
Your great exploits, your rare qualities;
Beloved by all the people, esteemed by the prince,
Son-in-law of the governor of all the province,
I do not reckon the title of my husband as anything to you:
That is a happiness for me which is not great for you;
But in view of your exploits, in view of your birth,
In view of your power, behold how crushed is our hope;

And abandon not to the hand of the executioner
What promises to our reasonable desire so noble a career.

Polyeucte.

I consider more; I know my advantages,
And the hope that great spirits base upon them.
They aspire in short only to fleeting blessings,
Which cares disturb, which dangers follow;
Death snatches them from us, fortune sports with them;
To-day on the throne, to-morrow in the mire;
And their highest splendor makes so many malcontents,
That few of your Cæsars have enjoyed them long.
I have ambition, but nobler and more beautiful:
This grandeur perishes, I wish an immortal one,
A happiness assured, without measure and without end,
Above envy, above fate.
Is it too much to buy it with a sad life,
Which soon, which suddenly, may be snatched from me:
Which gives me to enjoy only a fleeting moment,
And is not able to assure to me the one that follows it?

Pauline.

Behold the ridiculous fancies of your Christians;
Behold to what degree their falsehoods charm you:
All your blood is little for a happiness so sweet!
But is this blood yours to dispose of?
You have not life just as an heritage;
The day which gives it to you in the same time engages it:
You owe it to the prince, to the public, to the State.

23

Polyeucte.

I would wish to lose it for them in a battle;
I know what is the blessing of it and what is the glory of it.
They boast the memory of the ancestors of Decius;
And this name, precious still to your Romans,
At the end of six hundred years puts the empire in his hands.
I owe my life to the people, to the prince, to his crown;
But I owe it much more to the God who gives it to me.
If to die for one's prince is a glorious fate,
When one dies for his God, what a death will that be!

Pauline.

What a God

Polyeucte.

Gently, Pauline; He hears your words;
And He is not a God like your frivolous gods,
Senseless and deaf, powerless, mutilated,
Of wood, of marble, or of gold, as you wish them:
He is the God of the Christians, He is mine, He is yours;
And the earth and heaven know no other.

Pauline.

Adore Him in your soul, and give no sign of it.

Polyeucte.

That I should be, all at the same time, an idolater and a Christian!

Pauline.

Dissimulate only a moment: let Sévère depart,
And give the favor of my father opportunity to act.

Polyeucte.

The favor of my God is much more to be cherished;
He rescues me from perils that I might have incurred,
And without leaving me opportunity to turn back,
His favor crowns me on entering the race;
With the first gust of wind he brings me into port,
And when I come forth from baptism he sends me to death.
If you could comprehend both how little is life,
And by what pleasures this death is followed. . . . .
But what avails it to speak of these hidden treasures
To minds which God has not yet touched?

Pauline.

Cruel one! for it is time that my grief break forth,
And that a just reproach overwhelm an ungrateful soul!
Is that thy beautiful passion? are those thy vows?
Dost thou show the least affection for me?
I did not speak of the deplorable state
In which thy death will leave thy inconsolable wife;
I believed that love would speak of it enough to thee,
And I did not desire forced sentiments,
But that love so firm and so well merited
Which thou hadst promised me and which I have brought thee,
When thou wishest to leave me, when thou makest me die,

Can it draw from thee one tear, one sigh?
Thou leavest me, ingrate, and thou dost so with joy;
Thou dost not conceal it, thou wishest me to see it;
And thy heart, insensible to these sad attractions,
Imagines to itself a happiness where I shall not be!
That is then the surfeit that marriage brings?
I am odious to thee after having given myself!

Polyeucte.

Alas!

Pauline.

How much trouble that "alas" has to come out!
Yet, if it were the beginning of a happy repentance,
How many charms I would find in it, all forced as it is!
But courage, he is moved, I see tears flowing.

Polyeucte.

I shed some, and would to God that by means of shedding them
This too hardened heart might at least be pierced!
The deplorable state in which I leave you
Is very worthy of the tears which my love gives you;
And if one can feel any sorrows in heaven,
I will weep for you there over the excess of your misfortunes;
But if, in that abode of glory and of light,
That God altogether just and good can suffer my prayer;
If He deigns there to listen to a conjugal love,
Upon your blindness He will shed the light of day.
O Lord, from thy goodness I must obtain her;

She has too many virtues not to be a Christian :
It pleased thee to form her with too much merit
Not to know thee and not to love thee,
To live the unfortunate slave of hell,
And die as she was born under its sad yoke.

Pauline.

What dost thou say, unhappy man? what dost thou dare wish?

Polyeucte.

What I would wish to buy with all my blood.

Pauline.

Rather may . . . . !

Polyeucte.

It is vain that one seeks to defend oneself:
This God touches hearts when one least thinks of it.
This happy moment has not yet come;
It will come; but the time of it is not known to me.

Pauline.

Give up this chimera, and love me.

Polyeucte.

I love you,
Much less than my God, but much more than myself.

23*

Pauline.

In the name of this love, abandon me not.

Polyeucte.

In the name of this love, deign to follow my steps.

Pauline.

It is little to leave me, thou wishest then to beguile me?

Polyeucte.

It is little to go to heaven, I wish to lead thee thither.

Pauline.

Fancies!

Polyeucte.

Celestial verities!

Pauline.

Strange blindness!

Polyeucte.

Eternal brightness!

Pauline.

Thou preferrest death to the love of Pauline!

Polyeucte.

You prefer the world to divine favor!

Pauline.

Go, cruel one, go die; thou never lovedst me.

Polyeucte.

Live happy in the world, and leave me in peace.

Pauline.

Yes, I am going to leave thee in peace; trouble thyself no more
    about it;
I am going . . . . .

But at that moment Sévère enters. Fabian, as
usual, accompanies him. Supposing that he has
come to gloat over the downfall of her husband,
Pauline turns upon Sévère with a sharp reproach.
Polyeucte, however, at once undeceives her by explaining that he has himself requested Sévère to
visit him. He then makes a most extraordinary
proposition. This is nothing less than that Sévère
shall after the execution marry Pauline. A husband,
about to die, bequeaths his wife to his rival! Surely
this is the *ultima Thule* of altruism. Is such a propo-

sition in character? I think so. Polyeucte by a
mighty effort has subdued conjugal affection. All
his desire is for death. His eyes already catch the
brightness of the martyr's crown. His soul is in an
ecstasy of enthusiasm. How natural that he should
come to regard as an act of lofty Christian generosity
this relinquishment of his wife to the man who loved
her and whom she loved!

The renunciation serves, moreover, an important
purpose in the action of the piece by preparing the
way for the exquisite scene which follows.

When Polyeucte has concluded his astonishing
speech, he and his guards withdraw, leaving Sévère,
Pauline and Fabian together. Sévère after expressing his amazement at the course of Polyeucte, bursts
forth in the following passion-touched words:

" As for me, if my destiny, a little sooner propitious,
Had honored my devotion by marriage with you,
I should have adored only the splendor of your eyes;
Of them would I have made my kings, of them would I have
        made my gods;
Sooner would I have been reduced to dust, sooner would I have
        been reduced to ashes,
Than . . . . . "

But here Pauline checks this warm torrent of emotion which, like a geyser's stream, comes gushing up from his fervent heart.

" Let us break off there," she cries; "I fear lest I may hear too
        much,
And lest this warmth, which recalls your first fires,
May force on some sequel unworthy of us both.
Sévère, understand Pauline perfectly:
My Polyeucte touches on his last hour;
He has only a moment more before he dies;
You are the cause of it, though innocently.
I know not if your heart, open to your desires,
May have dared base any hope upon his destruction:
But know that there are no deaths so cruel
That to them I would not with firm brow wend my way,
That in hell there are no horrors that I would not endure,
Rather than soil a glory so pure,
Rather than-espouse, after his sad fate, a man
Who was in any way the cause of his death !
And, if you believe me of a heart so little sound,
The love that I had for you would all turn to hate.
You are generous; be so even to the end.
My father is in a state to grant you everything,
He fears you; and I risk this word further,
That, if he destroys my husband, it is to you that he sacrifices
        him.
Save this unfortunate, employ your influence in his behalf;

Exert yourself to serve him as a support.
I know that this is much that I ask;
But the greater the effort, the greater is the glory from it.
To rescue a rival of whom you are jealous,
That is a trait of virtue that belongs only to you;
And if your renown be not motive enough,
It is much that a woman, once so much beloved,
Should owe to your great heart what she has most dear:
Remember in short that you are Sévère.
Farewell. Determine alone what you ought to do;
If you are not such as I dare hope,
I wish not to know it that I may esteem you still."

What could be nobler than this reply? The words are exhaled from Pauline's pure soul, like sweet perfume from a spotless lily.

Not in all the dramatic literature of France shall we find a more beautiful character than this faithful wife. Pauline is worthy to claim sisterhood with Alcestis and Dido and Desdemona and Imogen.

Nor is Sévère less noble. He does not disappoint Pauline's hope. The next scene is an interview between him and his servant Fabian. Sévère, conquering his rebellious heart, determines to do his utmost to save his rival. Fabian warns his master against pursuing a course so full of peril.

"That advice," Sévère answers, "might be good for some com-
         mon soul.

Though he (Decius) holds in his hands my life and my fortune,

I am yet Sévère ; and all this great power

Is powerless over my glory and powerless over my duty.

Here honor constrains me, and I will satisfy it ;

Let fate afterwards show itself propitious or contrary,

As its nature is always inconstant,

Perishing glorious, I shall perish content.

I will tell thee much more, but under confidence,

The sect of the Christians is not what it is thought to be.

They are hated ; the reason I know not ;

And I see Decius unjust only in this regard.

From curiosity I have wished to become acquainted with them :

They are taken for sorcerers whose teacher is hell ;

And in this belief the punishment of death is visited

Upon secret mysteries that we do not understand.

But Eleusinian Ceres, and the good goddess,

Have like them their secrets at Rome and in Greece ;

Still we freely suffer in all places,

Their God alone excepted, every kind of god :

All the monsters of Egypt have their temples in Rome ;

Our ancestors at their will made a god of a man ;

And, their blood preserving their errors among us,

We fill heaven with all our Emperors :

But, to speak without disguise of so many apotheoses,

The effect of these metamorphoses is doubtful indeed.

The Christians have only one God, absolute master of all,

Whose mere will does all that he resolves :

But, if I dare say between us what seems to me true,
Our gods very often agree ill together;
And, were their wrath to crush me before your eyes,
We have a great many of them for them to be true gods.
Finally among the Christians morals are pure,
Vices are detested, virtues flourish;
They offer prayers for us who persecute them;
And during all the time since we have tormented them,
Has one seen them mutinous? has one seen them rebellious?
Have our princes had any more faithful soldiers?
Furious in war, they yield themselves up to our executioners,
And lions in combat, they die like lambs.
I have too much compassion for them not to defend them.
Come, let us find Félix; let us begin with his son-in-law;
And let us thus by a single action gratify
Pauline and my glory and my compassion."

What a broad, tolerant, judicial mind has Sévère. Had he lived some centuries later, he would have been an eloquent advocate of "soul liberty." He is just such a high heroic character as the noble Corneille loved to create. The glorious light that illuminates the features of Sévère emanates from the poet's own lofty mind. Sévère is admirable because Sévère is Corneille.

But we must hasten on to the conclusion of the drama. With the speech which we have just quoted, the fourth act closes. We are standing now in the shadow of the tragedy. The fifth act begins with a conversation between Félix and Albin. Cléon also is present but says nothing. Sévère has just been interceding with the governor in behalf of Polyeucte. Félix, however, suspects the generous young Roman of a treacherous design. This is not surprising. Base himself, Félix is quick to attribute baseness to others. Sévère, he thinks, hates him, disdains Pauline, and only intercedes for Polyeucte in order first to inveigle the luckless governor into a fatal error and then utterly crush him by bringing down upon him the Emperor's heavy displeasure. But Félix declares that he will thwart this deep laid plot. He will give Sévère himself a lesson in court intrigue. The governor seems to think that he is a master of Machiavellian politics.

But here again the consummate art of Corneille is clearly apparent. Like the scorpion, the crafty Félix girt by the fires of a false suspicion stings only himself. Nothing that Albin can say is able to dislodge this suspicion from his mind. He is intent on escaping the snare which he supposes that Sévère has set for him. He will not disobey the

24

Emperor by pardoning Polyeucte—not he. He is too shrewd for that. If Polyeucte still refuses to recant, then he shall die.

In the next scene Félix holds another colloquy with his son-in-law whom he has ordered to be brought before him again. The wily old courtier pretends to be secretly anxious to become a Christian himself, begs Polyeucte not to abandon him at a time in which he needs him so much as a guide, and earnestly urges him to dissimulate until Sévère shall have departed, when all will be well.

Polyeucte, however, at once detects the false ring in all this, and rebukes Félix for his deceitfulness. Nevertheless the governor still persists in his plea for guidance. Polyeucte in reply promises that on reaching heaven he will entreat the Lord, when thus face to face with Him, to bestow upon Félix the gift of faith.

Félix.

Thy loss, however, is going to plunge me into despair.

Polyeucte.

You have in your hands the wherewithal to repair it;
In taking from you one son-in-law, they give you another
Whose rank corresponds better with your own;
My loss is only an advantageous change for you.

Félix is enraged at "this insolence" as he calls it. Throwing off all disguise, he angrily bids Polyeucte choose between a return to paganism on the one hand and death on the other.

At this juncture Pauline enters. The scene which follows is highly interesting. Pauline tries once more to shake the purpose of her husband. But her tearful pleading is all in vain. Polyeucte is immovable. Then she turns to her father and makes a passionate appeal to his paternal love. Félix is deeply affected.

"Unhappy Polyeucte," he cries, "art thou alone insensible?
And dost thou wish alone to render thy crime unpardonable?
Canst thou see so many tears with an eye so careless?
Canst thou see so much love without being touched by it?"

It is with a tone of scorn that Polyeucte begins his reply. He is evidently quite disgusted with the shifts of Félix. The young Christian in the attempts to dissuade him from his purpose sees so many "ruses of hell." This is natural. The man is rapt to the highest pitch of religious enthusiasm. The rest of the scene is so sublime that we can not refrain from giving it all. After a momentary indignant outburst, Polyeucte continues thus:

"I adore one God, the master of the universe,

Under whom heaven, earth and hell tremble;

A God who, loving us with an infinite love,

Wished to die for us with ignominy,

And who by an effort of this excess of love,

Wishes to be offered as a victim for us each day.

But I am wrong to speak of Him to one who can not understand me.

Behold the blind error that you dare defend:

You stain all your gods with the blackest crimes;

You do not punish one of them which has not its teacher in
the skies;

Prostitution, adultery, incest,

Theft, assassination, and all that one detests,

That is the example that your immortals offer men to follow.

I have profaned their temple and broken their altars;

I would do it again, if I had it to do,

Even before the eyes of Félix, even before the eyes of Sévère,

Even before the eyes of the Senate, before the eyes of the
Emperor."

Félix.

At last my goodness yields to my just fury :

Worship them, or die.

Polyeucte.

I am a Christian.

Félix.

Impious wretch !

Worship them, I tell thee, or renounce life.

Polyeucte.

I am a Christian.

Félix.

Thou art!   O too obstinate heart!
Soldiers, execute the order that I have given.

Pauline.

Whither are you leading him?

Félix.

To death.

Polyeucte.

To glory.
Good-bye, dear Pauline; preserve my memory.

Pauline.

I will follow thee everywhere, and I will die if thou diest.

Polyeucte.

Follow not my steps, or give up your errors.

Félix.

Let him be taken out of my sight, and let my command be
obeyed.
Since he desires to perish, I consent that he perish.

24*

In this scene Corneille completes the character of Polyeucte. The statue is now finished "ad unguem." What a grand figure this Christian martyr makes! We forgive and forget his fanatical actions in the temple. We overlook his morbid asceticism. We think only of his present heroic attitude. He is about to die, willingly, proudly, joyfully, for his faith. Could the Christian's passionate love to God be more worthily represented? Polyeucte at once satisfies our minds, touches our hearts and commands our admiration. The dialogue at the end of the above scene is considered very fine by all critics.

" Ce mot, je suis chrétien, deux fois répété, égale," says Châteaubriand, " les plus beaux mots des Horaces."

Another inimitable stroke of genius is met a moment after in the following passage:

Pauline.

Où le conduisez-vous?

Félix.

À la mort.

Polyeucte.

À la gloire.

No Frenchman has ever mastered like Corneille this short-hand of emotion. The play is now nearly ended. The rest of the story may be told in a few words. Polyeucte is executed. Pauline, profoundly affected by her husband's sublime courage and cruel death, is suddenly converted to Christianity herself, and calls upon her father to kill her too. This change in the stricken widow, which is certainly fraught with pathetic interest, affords, we think, no ground for hostile criticism. Pauline is an unusually intelligent woman; it must have been next to impossible for her to exercise any real, vital faith in the pagan gods; the majestic divinity of her husband's words had doubtless impressed her deeply; her heart is melted by a great sorrow; what more favorable time could be found for the exercise of the enlightening, converting and vivifying power of the Holy Spirit. Both the psychology and the theology of the poet seem to be entirely correct.

We can not say the same about the conversion of Félix which occurs a few moments later. Sévère, shocked at the governor's cruelty, has just showered some very bitter reproaches upon him, and threatened him with heavy retribution. Félix is then instantaneously converted. Can we greatly blame the skeptical Voltaire for laughing at this? Is not Corneille piling Pelion upon Ossa in a rather unwarrantable fashion?

However, the dutiful heart of Pauline is charmed at the change in her father; Sévère, with his usual magnanimity, at once makes peace with the governor; and the black folds of the cloud that overhangs the death scene of the martyr are touched with the silvery light of promise. So ends " Polyeucte."

———

CHAPTER VII.

Final Estimate of Corneille: Fall of Classicism and Rise of Romanticism: Latest Developments.

IN this brochure we have said but little about the biography of Corneille. And this for the best of reasons. The great tragedist's life is written in his plays. His noble personality has been photographed upon his page by the sunlight of his genius. A few facts, however, should here be mentioned.

About 1640 Corneille married Marie de Lampérière, daughter of the Lieutenant-General of Andely; in 1647 the poet was elected to the Académie Française; in 1653 he stopped writing for the stage; in 1659, influenced by the persuasions of Fouquet, the Minister of Finance, he resumed dramatic composition; in 1663 the king granted him a pension; in 1674 he finally gave up the occupation of playwright; and in 1684, after

281

he had survived his faculties for a year, the curtain fell upon the last scene in the fifth act of the drama of his earthly life.

The following is a list of his plays with the date of each : Mélite (1629), Clitandre (1632), La Veuve (1633), La Galerie du Palais (1634), La Suivante (1634), La Place Royale (1635), Médée (1635), L'Illusion Comique (1636), Le Cid (1636), Horace (1639), Cinna (1639), Polyeucte (1640), La Mort de Pompée (1642), Le Menteur (1642), La Suite du Menteur (1644), Rodogune (1644), Théodore (1645), Heraclius (1647), Andromède (1650), Don Sanche d'Aragon (1650), Nicomède (1651), Pertharite (1653), Oedipe (1659), La Toison d'Or (1660), Sertorius (1662), Sophonisbe (1663), Othon (1664), Agésilas (1666), Attila (1667), Tite et Bérénice (1670), Pulchérie (1672), Suréna (1674). Psyché (1671) was the joint production of Molière, Corneille and Quinault.

We may obtain a good idea of how our poet looked from the interesting description of him which is given by Fontenelle. "M. Corneille," says he, "was quite large and quite full, very simple and common in appearance, always negligent and paying little attention to his exterior. He had quite an agreeable countenance, a large nose, a pretty mouth, eyes full of fire, an animated physiognomy and very marked features, well adapted to be transmitted to posterity by a medallion or a bust. His pronunciation was not altogether clear; he read his verses with force, but without grace."

His disposition was melancholy. His manners were brusque; sometimes he even appeared rude. But in reality few men have had kinder or more generous hearts.

He was, to quote Fontenelle again, "a good father, a good husband, a good relative, tender and full of friendship."

His conversation, La Bruyère declares, was "tiresome." Corneille was not skilled in the use of the light simitar of repartee; his weapon was the broadsword of lofty dialectics.

He is far from being the only great author deficient in conversational powers. A number of famous names will at once occur to the reader—Vergil, Descartes, La Fontaine, Addison, Dryden, and that other delightful author, Goldsmith,

"who wrote like an angel and talked like poor Poll."

When Corneille's friends censured him for not remedying this defect, he replied with a smile:

"I am not the less Pierre Corneille."

In matters of business the poet was a mere child, utterly unpractical and entirely incapable of taking care of the money which he earned by his pen. This is the prime cause of his poverty in his old age.

One other trait of his character deserves especial notice. He was a sincere Christian. The great poet whose works, like a vein of gold in a bed of quartz, shall endure as long as the language in which they are written, bowed with a humility that degraded not, before the Judge of all the earth.

If it be asked what was the historic function that Corneille performed, we may answer that he banished bad taste from the theatre, that he quickened with the touch of life the chaotic theatrical materials which he found at his coming, that he divined, developed and determined the classical drama, and that he peopled the French stage with heroic characters whom he idealized from real life, bestowing true passions upon them and causing them to give to the age object lessons in ethical science. He exerted a powerful influence upon both departments of dramatic art.

By writing "Le Cid," he created the true classical tragedy; by writing "Le Menteur" he created the comedy of manners and gave the cue which brought upon the stage an author worthy to stand with covered head as an equal in the presence of such masters of the comedian's art as Aristophanes and Shakspeare.

Molière himself freely acknowledged his great debt to Corneille. Speaking, in a letter to Boileau, of "Le Menteur," the great comedian said: "When it was first performed, I had already a wish to write, but was in doubt as to what it should be. My ideas were still confused, but this piece determined them. In short, but for the appearance of 'Le Menteur,' though I should no doubt have written comedies of intrigue, like *l'Étourdi* or *le Dépit amoureux*, I should perhaps never have written *le Misanthrope*."

This frank acknowledgment does as much honor to Molière as to Corneille. Only a truly great heart would be so generous.

25

The style of Corneille is remarkable for its inequality. This peculiarity has never been more happily indicated than by Molière. "My friend Corneille," said he, "has a familiar who inspires him with the finest verses in the world. But sometimes the familiar leaves him to shift for himself and then he fares very badly." Nothing could be more delicate or more apt.

Corneille was a great admirer of Lucan, whose *Pharsalia* he had, when a young man, translated in whole or in part. His careful study of that poem has left an indelible impress upon his own works. He was undoubtedly attracted to the Roman bard by the subtle affinity of similar genius. So marked are the resemblances between the styles of the two authors that many of the adjectives employed in a brief enumeration of the qualities of one must be used in epitomizing the qualities of the other.

Does Quintilian speak of Lucan as "ardens et concitatus et sententiis clarissimus?" We can say the same of Corneille. Is Lucan unequal, declamatory, sometimes bombastic? So is Corneille. Is the critical reader of *Pharsalia* offended at the Roman poet's evident straining after effect? Examples of the same overwrought rhetoric may be found in *La Mort de Pompée*. The writer of this sketch hopes to find the time at some future day to draw up a somewhat elaborate comparison of the two poets, illustrating it by copious citations from each. For our present purpose, however, the above passing reference will suffice.

Corneille's genius was a limited genius—limited in its innate powers, limited by the clanking chains of the unities, and limited by the poet's own action in choosing all his subjects from one small segment in the great circle of human passions. He loved to represent upon the stage not the weak and yielding elements of our nature, but the strong, the firm, the resisting elements. Hence he is always appealing to the sentiment of admiration. Is this a proper principle on which to base a tragedy? Boileau says not. Critics, in plenty, after Boileau say not. But it is, perhaps, quite sufficient in reply to them all to say that admiration in the form of hero-worship has time and time again proved itself a powerful factor in the history of the world; that the roots of this hero-worship are entwined with our strongest passions; and that the sentiment of admiration aroused by the perusal of biographies of the world's great has kindled in the hearts of the young in every land and every age an intense desire to imitate the high exploits of which they have read. It would seem that the excitation of such an emotion was well adapted to produce the noblest effects of tragedy. At any rate these heroic themes were exactly suited to the genius of Corneille. He belongs by nature to the ideal school of dramatists. He has abstracted from human nature, as concreted in the actual, all those noble qualities that glorify our race, and has, by the exercise of his creative imagination, recombined them into sublime characters whose colossal figures tower above all the weakness and wickedness and weariness of real life. His writings are thus in the highest degree wholesome. We can not conceive how an intelligent person can attentively peruse one of our poet's masterpieces without experiencing emotions which themselves exert an influence at once purifying and fructifying upon the moral nature.

The majestic personality of Corneille pervades his works. In them we find a sublime man uttering his sublime thoughts in sublime words. The nervous vigor of his descriptions is worthy of the highest praise. He intuitively selects the essential elements of a scene, transfers them to his canvas with a few rapid strokes of his brush, and in a moment the whole is pictured before us with a fidelity to nature, a clearness of outline, and a vividness of color that bespeak the master.

Yet Corneille had his defects. There is sometimes too much of the hyper-heroic, too much of the super-human in his characters. They would be a good deal greater, if they were not quite so great. They are like Dante's tower which

> " firmly set,
> Shakes not its top for any blast that blows."

Perhaps we should like them better, if they resembled more the giant oak which bends and groans, but breaks not beneath the wild power of the tempest.

Often, also, these characters are too self-conscious. They have a full appreciation of their own bravery, magnanimity and virtue. Their frequent assertion of their various excellencies jars upon the reader like a sharp discord in a soul-stirring symphony. Excessive self-consciousness is manifested in another

25*

way by Corneille's characters. In moments when we should expect to see them convulsed and contorted with passion, we find them in comparative calmness dissecting and defining their emotions according to the introspective method of the rational psychologists and with the precision of trained logicians. Thus long sections of conscious declamation frequently usurp the place that should be occupied by the "disjecta membra" of passionate speech. The declamatory passages, it is true, are of the finest quality, "Sed nunc non erat his locus." Instead of these critical analyses of emotion, the poet should have given us the concussion and conflagration of emotion in synthesis.

We shall mention only one other fault of our author. He never succeeded in completely purging his writings of the affected gallantry, the fantastic euphuism, the "faux brillant" of his times. As we behold him struggling to burst the earthy bondage of bad taste, it makes us think of Milton's lion, "pawing to get free." The spectacle is one to excite admiring sympathy rather than contemptuous criticism.

Often the question is asked, which was the greater dramatist, Corneille or Racine? One may answer in metaphor. As we cast our eyes over the famous fields of French literature, we see yonder a silvery winding river, reflecting in its crystal flood the fleecy clouds, and singing a love song to the flowers on its banks, as it glides onward. And over there we see a majestic mountain towering up above all things near, rugged; sublime; with deep precipices and jagged peaks; girt round anon with storm-clouds in which the lightnings flash and the thunders crash and roll; but bearing aloft, above the storm, his kingly head with its jewelled diadem which glitters and glows in heaven's own light. The winding river is Jean Racine; the majestic mountain is *Le Grand Corneille*. And so we take our leave of him.

A few brief words in explanation of the high excellence attained by the French in the drama, a hurried recapitulation of some of the reasons why Classicism became dominant in the seventeenth century, a meagre sketch of the development of Romanticism, and we shall have reached the limit which we have set for ourselves in this book.

The French drama is the consummate flower of French literature. Upon this point all critics are agreed, whether they belong to that too numerous band of carping censors who, looking through the deeply colored spectacles of national prejudice and national antipathy upon a master-piece of Corneille or Racine, vent themselves in vitriolic sarcasm because its brightness then seems dimmed and its beauty blurred, or whether they be members of that other extreme and extravagant class who esteem the stage of Paris above that of Athens itself, and hail Victor Hugo as a scion of the lineage of Shakspeare.

It is no very difficult task to name some, at least, of the causes which have concurred to make the drama the highest expression of the literary genius of France.

The typical Frenchman has an instinctive knowledge of scenic effect born in him as the natural concomitant of his Celtic blood; that quick, keen, flashing wit which we call *l'esprit Gaulois* is another of his birthrights; the Latin logic wrought into the mental tissue of his ancestors has been transmitted by heredity to him; the forces of his nature are so

closely correlated that the white light of thought
can, in a moment, be converted into electric emotion; he has a passion for proportion, an artist's
reverence for perfect form, and a courtier's regard
for decorum; he worships glory; he will fight for
an idea; in short his whole being is saturated with
the very essence of drama. It is for this reason
that French history, from first to last, is a thrilling
tragedy, a piquant comedy, or a roaring farce. What
wonder that the authors of such a nation should
achieve their most brilliant triumphs in the domain
of dramatic composition?

Since each successive age is the outgrowth and
resultant of all the ages past, bound to them by a
connection at once necessary, natural and organic,
determined by their character and dowered with
their wealth, we must study schools of literature in
their history, in their origin and evolution, and in
their logical and psychological relations to preceding schools.

Especially is this true of a literature which presents such a striking continuity of development as
does the French. From the time of the trouvères,
who in their *chansons de geste* celebrated high-souled

heroes' daring deeds and mingled love's melodious
music with the horrid din of war, to the days of
those " literary brigands " with long hair and grotesque costume who fought under the standard that
Hugo raised, there have been in French literature no
real stoppages in the cyclical movement of progress,
no breaks in the curve of change, no gaps in the
order of succession.

Revolutions, indeed, there have been, but each
revolution was merely a stage of a larger evolution.
One must, therefore, examine the French theatre
according to the scientific method, seeking to discover the sources of the drama and to trace its
development, bearing ever in mind the characteristics of the French people, studying the environment
physical, political and ethical by which they have
been surrounded, and noting carefully the creative,
formative, dominant spirit of the epochs investigated.

We have seen how the different varieties of drama
succeeded one another upon the French stage; let us
now try to account for the prevalence of Classicism
in the seventeenth century. The central figure in
the literary history of France during the early part
of that century is the poet Malherbe, the tyrant of

words and syllables. He is the lapidary on whose wheel French words, like precious gems, were cut and polished until they were ready to be set in the crowns of the kingly company of authors now about to appear. He strenuously insists upon a pure diction, a simple style and a finished versification. He is the prophet of good taste.

Next to him should be named the letter-writer and essayist, Balzac, who did for prose what Malherbe had done for poetry. Balzac's style is dignified, harmonious and periodic. He set the standard of elegant prose composition. These writers were the two cotyledons of Classicism.

Against the school of literary reform founded by Malherbe and Balzac, were arrayed two powerful influences imported into France from abroad.

The first of these came from Italy. In 1615, the Italian poet Marino, upon the invitation of the minister of Marie de Medici, visited Paris, reëstablished there a troupe of Italian comedians, and introduced into France that affected style which corresponds to the Euphuism of Lilly in the history of English letters. The influence of Marino and his disciples was immense both on literature and life.

The other foreign influence came from the land of Don Quixote. Of the effect of the introduction of this Spanish element into French society and French letters, we have already spoken. The Italian and the Spanish influences met and mingled in the Hôtel de Rambouillet. The cultured company who met here did much to mould the style of the drama. Their potent influence was exerted on the side of Classicism whose rigid propriety fitted in exactly with their ideas of social form. Another power in literature was the French Academy, created by Richelieu about 1629.[1]

The seventeenth century had received from the sixteenth a decided bent in the direction of classical culture. The momentum acquired in the preceding two hundred years was augmented by the untiring labors of the scholars of the seventeenth century. The great past continued to be regarded with profoundest reverence. During the second quarter of the century the canons of classical literature were

[1] The Academy was not founded by law until some years later. The king granted letters patent early in 1635; but it was getting on toward the autumn of 1637 before the Parliament would give its consent to the establishment of the new society.

established as the supreme law to which every French writer must yield obedience. It was the function of the Academy to formulate, expound and vindicate these canons. How thoroughly it did its work, is known to all students of French history.

Nor should we forget the profound effect produced upon literature by the philosophy of the age. Idealism awakened men to a vivid consciousness of their relations to God, taught Claude Gelée to paint "the light that never was on sea or land," and touched the eye of poetry with a wonderful ointment which disclosed untold treasures to her view. The influence of Descartes, the day-star of modern philosophy, permeated the intellectual activities of the period.

It was during the latter half of the century that literature attained its most perfect development. All causes coöperated to strengthen the ascendency of Classicism in the drama.

Unity was the characteristic of the age. Protestantism had been silenced. All religious authority was wielded by one supreme pontiff. The power of the nobility had been broken. All political

26

authority was vested in the king. *"L'état, c'est moi"* is the key-note of the reign of Louis XIV.

The forms of etiquette were observed with the utmost strictness. Everything must be done according to rule. Fashion was a goddess to whom every knee must bend. Decorum was the first thought in the minds of all the fine lords and ladies who, bedecked in perrukes and powder and fuss and feathers, sat listening to the great plays of Corneille, Racine and Molière. An instinct for regularity was everywhere apparent. Now this unity, this decorum, this regularity are the salient features in the classic drama. Very naturally, then, that style of drama came into undisputed possession of the stage.

We can not tarry to sketch even in vaguest outline the glories of the theatre in the Age of Louis Quatorze. Adequately to do so would require a treatise in itself. We must instead hasten on to our only remaining task, that of indicating the reasons for the decline of Classicism and the rise of Romanticism.

The eighteenth century in French letters was the trough between two silver-crested billows, the seventeenth century on the one hand and the nineteenth

on the other. The drama sank far below the lofty
height to which it had risen in the works of the
immortal trio of the preceding age. Racine had
imitated the Greeks. Voltaire imitated Racine.
A whole spawn of dullards imitated Voltaire. Art
became artifice; skilfully drawn characters glowing
with the warmth of human passion gave place to
pale abstractions declaiming the dogmas of encyclopaedism; imagination was imprisoned behind the
iron bars of form; dramatists were threshing over
and over the straw of a long past harvest; all was
as inane as it was urbane. The theatre of Racine
is a flower-garden; the theatre of Voltaire is a
brilliant display of cut flowers in antique vases; the
theatre of Briffaut is an herbarium.

If we look closely at the eighteenth century we
can see, wise prophets after the event as we are, a
number of forces all working together to produce
the literary revolution of the next age. A sensational psychology, deep-rooted in the fertile and
friendly soil of the French mind, is about to bear
its full and bitter fruitage of atheism in philosophy,
utilitarianism in morals, conventionalism in art and
corruption in life. Encyclopaedism is striving to

tear off the Pope's tiara, and shatter the sceptre of the king. It is a period of reaction, a period of transition, a period of fire-producing friction. Gross materialism murders all the fine instincts of the soul. Our poor clay body with its frailties, its appetites and its passions is mistaken for the whole of man, indulged with every sensual pleasure, and fed upon all varieties of forbidden fruit. Then comes the great Revolution with those bloody orgies at which all Europe trembled and turned pale. Crime holds high carnival in Paris. Men become wonted to the sight of the most horrible physical suffering. Death slays his prey in every street. The gleam of the guillotine's knife, the terrified, distorted features of the victim, the prayers, the shrieks, the spurting flow of crimson, are all familiar to every citizen. We can well understand how a nation whose natures have been thus accustomed to turmoil and turbulence and massacre, whose nerves have been steeled in the atrocities of civil strife, and whose sensibilities have been deadened by dreadful sights and sounds, should soon demand sensational dramas on the stage.

When we examine the literary activities of the eighteenth century we find three other influences which were important factors in the preparation for Romanticism. Scholars are giving themselves with sympathetic enthusiasm to the study of the Middle Ages. Shakspeare, though not yet recognized as the Igdrasil of literature, is translated by Letourneur and Ducis and begins to find admirers not a few. Rousseau, falling passionately in love with nature and tinting his prose with the rainbow hues of poetry, introduces into literature the new element of sentimentality. His disciple, St. Pierre, burns incense upon the same altar. Beautiful landscapes, scenes of Arcadian innocence and the delights of idyllic life are described by him with splendid eloquence. Thus arose a literary cult for the worship of nature. Early in the nineteenth century the tide of tendency toward Romanticism becomes much stronger.

Two sets of influences are clearly discernible, the one foreign, the other domestic. German literature begins to be read in translations. The weird imagination of Hoffmann, the full-orbed genius of Goethe and the dramatic power of Schiller fired French writers with a longing for something better than the insipid commonplaces of effete Classicism.

26*

This taste for German letters was greatly stimulated by the writings of Mme. de Staël. Banished from Napoleon's court, she had been cordially welcomed into the inner circles of literary, artistic and philosophical life. She interprets Germany to France. Her *De l'Allemagne* is an *aqua regia* holding in solution the golden thoughts of the German romanticists. The fifteenth chapter, *De l'art dramatique*, deserves to be especially noted because of its great reformatory effect upon French tragedy. So much for German influence.

From England came another literary inundation. The world-wide, heaven-high, ocean-deep Shakspeare was studied with increasing appreciation. Scott, who had reconstructed the Middle Ages and pictured feudalism in all its splendor, became exceedingly popular. Byron, misanthropic, pessimistic and despairing, captured the fancy of all France by the vivid coloring of his " Satanic " poems, as they were then called, and produced a profound impression especially upon the rising generation.

Our country, too, contributed some motive force to the revolution. The fresh, virile, thrilling novels of Cooper, whose style is racy of the soil, fascinated by their fine descriptions both ignorant and learned.

As the commingled waters of these three invading floods recede, they overlay the fields of French literature with a rich loam of genius which lies at the roots of the gorgeous, if somewhat rank efflorescence of Romanticism.

Look now for a moment at the domestic influences. *André Chenier*, a brave young poet guillotined by *Robespierre* in 1794, had been dead a quarter of a century when above his grave his poetry first unclosed its clustered buds and stood revealed in all the freshness and richness and lustre of its Greek beauty. Classic in form, he was romantic in spirit, and his works enchanted young France.

Much more potent is the influence of *Château-briand*, the leader of the great Catholic reaction, the defender of Christianity as the *alma mater* of the fine arts, the literary Midas at whose magic touch the Middle Ages turn to golden splendor, the eloquent interpreter of Gothic architecture and the prose poet of nature, who was for many years the Zeus of the French Parnassus. From him more than from any other one man in the beginning did

Romanticism receive its kinetic energy. Château-
briand is the sponsor of Hugo.

The only other writer who thus, without being a
member of the Romantic school, exerted a formative
influence upon it was *Lamartine.* He rejects all
the machinery of Classicism, places his aeolian lyre
at the open window of his soul, and seeks to make
the wandering winds of thought and passion and
reverie utter themselves in mellifluous music. He
renders into words the vague emotions that arise
within us when we muse on nature, infinitude and
the spirit world. He is Christian, he is modern,
he is sentimental. His descriptions are exceedingly
faithful. In the limpid depth of his verse the
features of nature are as clearly reflected as were
the rocks and firs and argent moon in the lake of
which he sings. He is the link of transition between
the old and the new poetry.

Let us now take a hasty glance at the condition
of things in the domain of thought. For the first
few years of the century the sensationalism of
Condillac continues to dominate philosophy. Then
three powerful knights, Royer-Collard, Maine de
Biran and Victor Cousin, displaying on their lances

the colors of *spiritualisme*, enter the lists to do battle
as champions of a nobler creed. Though thus
vigorously attacked, the defenders of materialism are,
however, making a stubborn resistance. Encyclopaedism has infiltrated the French mind. It is not
surprising that from this sensational philosophy
should issue a sensational drama. The methods
and results of science were perverted to the propa-
gation of "the gospel of dirt." Men ever working
in matter, ever studying the properties of matter,
never looking above matter, easily become material-
ists. They forget that physical science is not all
science; they demand that everything shall be
demonstrated to the senses; they turn a deaf ear
to intuition; they repudiate God and worship the
golden calf of utilitarianism. We must especially
note that the quest of science, whether she be investi-
gating the tiniest organism or the largest planet,
is from first to last emphatically a quest for fact.
It is proved fact that forms the foundation of the
positive philosophy already adumbrated in the early
lectures of Comte. The realism of the Romantic
school is the projection of this same scientific method
upon the line of literary art.

In political affairs after 1824 there is a deal of fermentation. Monarchism is wrestling with republicanism. The grandfathers of this generation had fought for the rights of man : the grandsons, inheriting a hatred of tyranny, could ill brook the high-handed course of Charles X. The third estate has now "become something." Civilization has hewn broad the path for the onward march of democracy. Political economists are weaving socialistic theories for the relief of the toiling masses. A king sits upon the throne, but the love of freedom reigns in the nation's heart.

What could be more natural than that such a generation, ready to revolt against the despotism of the Bourbons, should be equally ready to revolt against the despotism of the classics? What more natural than that liberalism in politics should go hand in hand with liberalism in letters?

This period was distinguished, also, for a widespread passion for history. The Middle Ages were invested with a glamour of romance, Gothic architecture became the fashion, and antique furniture was sought after with an earnestness somewhat ludicrous. The effect of such enthusiasm for the

past was felt in all departments of literature, and
is seen in the large number of plays which the
romanticists produced in their effort to portray
famous characters of history precisely as they
were and amid all the lights and shades of local
color.

Nor must we forget the great enlargement of the
reading public consequent upon the rise of the
bourgeoisie, the transference of power to the third
estate and the successful struggle of the working
classes for political rights. Democracy in letters
followed in the wake of democracy in the state. A
dramatist addressed no longer, as in former ages,
a select circle of aristocrats, courtiers and punctilious
devotees of fashion. He had to appeal to the great
assemblage of the people where culture indeed was
to be found, but where deplorable ignorance far
more abounded, where the esthetic tastes of the
many were comparatively low, and where the im-
portunity of the senses too often stifled the aspirations of the spirit. The masses who could not
appreciate the chaste beauty of a classic masterpiece,
but who were delighted with the coarse emotions
of the circus, welcomed with applause the highly

seasoned plays of the romanticists, which were often melodramatic, gross and immoral.

Having thus briefly reviewed the causes that led to Romanticism, we may now ask what, in the light of history, were the distinctive characteristics of this movement? Nor is the question difficult to answer. Romanticism according to the professions of its partisans was to be a battle for liberty in literature; a struggle of the modern concept of the discordant dualism of man's nature against the ancient concept of the harmonious synergy of all his faculties; an attempt to substitute the poetry of Teutonic melancholy, with its ever present suggestions of the life immortal, for the poetry of Greek joyousness with its sublimated sensualism; and, finally, an effort to vitalize art by infusing into it new blood, to lead genius forth into wider fields, and to represent life with such minute accuracy as should make one hear the *ventre Saint gris* of Henri IV and see the very wart on Cromwell's rugged face.

The writers of the new school are to translate the "varied language" that nature speaks. Melpomene is to seek inspiration from the scroll of Clio. The Middle Ages whose sublime architecture is " frozen music," poetry in stone and Christianity in symbol, are to be carefully studied, appreciated at their full value, and restored to the mind's eye by the pen of the novelist and the playwright. The romanticists are to give expression to the infinite aspirations of the Christian faith, re-echo the noble sentiments of chivalry and put themselves in touch with troubadour and trouvère.

As a matter of fact, however, the productions of the new school in France fail to exhibit any such excellence as one might naturally look for after so stirring a manifesto. We shall reach a better understanding of the net results in the drama by contrasting the classic and the romantic styles. Each has its peculiar merits, each its peculiar defects. The classic drama is statuesque; the romantic drama is picturesque; the former presents us with beauty of contour, the latter with beauty of color; the one is idealistic, soaring to the true above us, the other is realistic seeking rather the true about us; the great dramatists of the seventeenth century never mingle sorrow and mirth in the same piece, the playwrights of the nineteenth century have married the comic to the serious and the grotesque to the sublime; the

27

verse of the classicists flows along with an unbroken murmur of monotonous music, the verse of the romanticists breaks into discordant yet not unpleasing ripples round reefs of *enjambement*; the classic drama emphasizes the psychological side of passion, the romantic drama emphasizes the physiological side; the school of Corneille bow before the three unities as the Greeks before the three fates, the school of Hugo are iconoclastic, breaking without compunction the fetiches of the past; the classic poet dips his patera "heavy with gems and gold" into the sparkling waters of Aganippe, the romantic poet drinks with his horn which is golden, too, long draughts from Mimer's fountain.

Let us notice now the decline of the two schools. Classicism, cast down from the sun-kissed domicile of genius into the Mamertine dungeon of imitation, became the mere emaciated and emasculated skeleton of its former self. But, though it sank low and yet lower, it never outraged the proprieties. Its slavish decorum was its bane. Upon play after play we may write our verdict: "faultily faultless, icily regular, splendidly null." Romanticism, on the contrary, scoffing at rules and seeking the unusual, the striking, the fantastic, the monstrous in nature, soon earned the title of "La littérature extravagante." Good morals were scandalized and good taste was shocked by plays in which sensuality with brazen assurance stalked upon the stage, and in which vulgarity was thinly veneered with wit, and mortal sins plated with tinsel poetry. "Whatever we paint," cried the romanticists, "we will paint not as it ought to be, but as it is, and we will paint everything that is in nature." "*L'art pour l'art*" is the countersign of their camp.

From this embryonic germ, by the most natural process in the world was developed French *Realism* —a variety of literature very different from that American type which goes under the same title and which describes for us the courtship and marriage of Miss Mediocrity and Mister Everyday, both residents of the town of Humdrum. American Realism is generally harmless, if insipid; French Realism too often, alas, too often hides the serpent of sin beneath a bank of flowers. Real life is, it may be, portrayed, but what sort of real life? Seldom, indeed, the life of virtue, honor and duty. The realist scarcely ever makes any attempt to depict the "sweetness and light" that fill the homes of so many millions of men. He prefers to uncover the worm in the rose, the cancer in the bosom of society and the evil passions seething in the caldron of the desperately wicked heart.

Realism dyed some shades darker becomes Naturalism. For the writers of this school there is no good, there is no bad, there is only the true. The playwright is a scientist. He invents nothing. He merely observes, experiments and draws up his report of what he has seen, analyzed and explained. He practices a sort of psychological vivisection; he is learned in the anatomy of motive; he has a passion for the pathology of crime. The horrible, the diabolical, the uncanny fascinate him. Note-book in hand he visits the hospital, jail and morgue, gathering documentary evidence upon which to base his scientific demonstration showing how the character of this or that personage is the resultant of the coaction or counteraction of heredity and environment. This, then, is the final development of Romanticism; this the nadir of its degradation. *The clammy fingers of Empiricism are choking the soul out of art.*

Oh, France, beautiful France, dear sister republic who now art bravely bearing aloft the torch of Freedom in the world beyond the seas, rear no longer the apples of Sodom in thy garden of literature; dash to earth that poisoned chalice which an irreligious art is holding to thy lips; turn away from the men with muck rakes; lift thine eyes to the glorious orbs that glitter in thy firmament of intellect; feast thy soul upon the grandeur of Corneille, the beauty of Racine, the wit of Molière; strive for the ideal; let thy art become a ladder which shall reach from earth to heaven and on which thou shalt see the angels of God descending and ascending. Thus shalt thou take in literature thy rightful rank as a leader among the nations, guiding them onward toward the TRUE and upward toward the GOOD!

" May these things be ! "

THE END.